Here's all the great literature in this grade level of *Celebrate Reading!*

B O O K A

"Mom, Mom, My Ears Are Growing!"

And Other Joys of the Real World

Bingo Brown, Gypsy Lover
from the novel by
Betsy Byars
✸ *School Library Journal* Best Book
✸ ALA Notable Children's Book

The Cybil War
from the novel by
Betsy Byars
✸ ALA Notable Children's Book
✸ Children's Choice

Remarkable Children
from the book by
Dennis Brindell Fradin

And Still I Rise
from the collection by
Maya Angelou
✸ *School Library Journal* Best Book

How It Feels to Fight for Your Life
from the book by
Jill Krementz
✸ Outstanding Science Trade Book
✸ Teachers' Choice

Fast Sam, Cool Clyde, and Stuff
from the novel by
Walter Dean Myers
✸ Children's Choice

The Summer of the Falcon
from the novel by
Jean Craighead George
✸ Newbery Medal Author

Featured Poet
Maya Angelou

BOOK B

Look Both Ways

Seeing the Other Side

B O O K C

Free to Fly

A User's Guide to the Imagination

Theo Zephyr
from the novel by
Dean Hughes
✷ Children's Choice

The People Could Fly: American Black Folktales
from the collection by
Virginia Hamilton
Illustrations by Leo and
Diane Dillon
✷ *New York Times* Best Illustrated
✷ ALA Notable Children's Book

Joyful Noise: Poems for Two Voices
from the collection by
Paul Fleischman
✷ Newbery Medal

The Town Cat and Other Tales
from the collection by
Lloyd Alexander
✷ Newbery Medal Author
✷ American Book
Award Author

The Foundling and Other Tales of Prydain
from the collection by
Lloyd Alexander
✷ *School Library Journal*
Best Book

Cinderella Finds Time
by Val R. Cheatham

In Search of Cinderella
by Shel Silverstein
✷ ALA Notable Children's Book

Glass Slipper
by Jane Yolen
✷ Kerlan Award Author

...And Then the Prince Knelt Down and Tried to Put the Glass Slipper on Cinderella's Foot
by Judith Viorst
✷ Christopher Award Author

Yeh Shen: A Cinderella Story from China
retold by Ai-Ling Louie
Illustrations by Ed Young
✷ ALA Notable Children's Book

Featured Poets
Paul Fleischman
Pat Mora
Shel Silverstein
Jane Yolen
Judith Viorst

B O O K D

Journey Home

and Other Routes to Belonging

Apple Is My Sign
by Mary Riskind
- ALA Notable Children's Book
- Notable Social Studies Trade Book

The Circuit
by Francisco Jiménez

The American Family Farm
from the photo essay by George Ancona and Joan Anderson
- ALA Notable Children's Book
- Notable Social Studies Trade Book

A Jar of Dreams
from the novel by Yoshiko Uchida
- Children's Choice
- Notable Social Studies Trade Book

Journey Home
from the novel by Yoshiko Uchida
- Children's Choice
- Notable Social Studies Trade Book

My People, the Sioux
from the autobiography by Chief Luther Standing Bear

The Lost Garden
from the autobiography by Laurence Yep
- Newbery Honor Author

Featured Poets
Gwendolyn Brooks
Edwin Muir

Arriving Before I Start

Passages Through Time

Max and Me and the Time Machine
from the novel by Gery Greer and Bob Ruddick
✹ *School Library Journal* Best Book

Journey to Technos
by Claire Boiko

The Day the Mountain Blew Apart
by Chris Copeland

Pompeii: Nightmare at Midday
by Kathryn Long Humphrey

Tails of the Bronx
from the collection by Jill Pinkwater

Children of the Wild West
from the book by Russell Freedman
✹ ALA Notable Children's Book
✹ Notable Social Studies Trade Book
✹ Teachers' Choice

Great Summer Olympic Moments
from the book by Nate Aaseng

Maya Ballplayers
by Peter Kvietok

B O O K F

Just Like a Hero

Talk About Leadership

The Revenge of the Incredible Dr. Rancid and His Youthful Assistant, Jeffrey
from the novel by
Ellen Conford
✷Young Readers' Choice Award Author

The Gold Coin
by Alma Flor Ada
✷Christopher Award

Mother Teresa
from the biography by
Patricia Reilly Giff

Prince of the Double Axe
by Madeleine Polland

Featured Poet
John Greenleaf Whittier

Celebrate Reading! Trade Book Library

Our Sixth-Grade Sugar Babies
by Eve Bunting
- *School Library Journal* Best Book

Goodbye, Chicken Little
by Betsy Byars
- Children's Choice
- Children's Editors' Choice
- Library of Congress Children's Book
- *New York Times* Notable Book

Dragon of the Lost Sea
by Laurence Yep
- ALA Notable Children's Book
- International Reading Association 100 Favorite Paperbacks of 1989

The Westing Game
by Ellen Raskin
- Newbery Medal
- Boston Globe-Horn Book Award

The Brocaded Slipper and Other Vietnamese Tales
by Lynette Vuong

The Jedera Adventure
by Lloyd Alexander
- Parents' Choice

The Endless Steppe: Growing Up in Siberia
by Esther Hautzig
- ALA Notable Children's Book
- Boston Globe-Horn Book Award Honor Book
- Lewis Carroll Shelf Award

Baseball in April and Other Stories
by Gary Soto
- ALA Notable Children's Book
- *Parenting* Reading-Magic Award

Tom's Midnight Garden
by Philippa Pearce
- Carnegie Medal Winner

The House of Dies Drear
by Virginia Hamilton
- ALA Notable Children's Book

Journey to Jo'burg: A South African Story
by Beverly Naidoo
- Notable Social Studies Trade Book

Jackie Joyner-Kersee
by Neil Cohen

Arriving Before I Start

Passages Through Time

Titles in This Set

"Mom, Mom, My Ears Are Growing!"

Look Both Ways

Free to Fly

Journey Home

Arriving Before I Start

Just Like a Hero

About the Cover Artist
Wayne McLoughlin lives in Vermont with his wife Jackie and his daughter Allison. He has illustrated several books for children and writes humorous stories for *Field and Stream Magazine.*

ISBN 0-673-81170-0

1997
Scott, Foresman and Company, Glenview, Illinois

Printed in the United States of America.

Acknowledgments appear on page 144.

12345678910DQO10099989796

Arriving Before I Start

Passages Through Time

ScottForesman
A Division of HarperCollins*Publishers*

CONTENTS

DESTINATION

New York City and the West!

DESTINATION

The Games!

Student Resources

Enter
our time
POCKET RACER
6

machine

Travel back in time and test your strength against the Earl of Hampshire's champion. Slip into a universe caught in the stranglehold of the Supreme Technocrat. Strap yourself in. Sit back. WE'RE OFF!!

FROM *MAX AND ME AND THE TIME MACHINE*

HOW I FACED THE HAMPSHIRE MAULER

by Gery Greer
and Bob Ruddick

I guess I'm like everybody else. When I do something that's pretty terrific, I expect to get some credit for it. A little praise, a pat on the back, a bit of wild, thunderous applause —maybe even a chorus of "Bravo! Fantastic! Way to go!"

And that's just what I was expecting when I hauled that huge crate into our clubhouse and told my best friend, Max Zilinski, that it contained a time machine I had picked up at a garage sale down the street. For $2.50.

But Max did not applaud. He snorted.

"Who're you trying to kid, Steve?" he said, barely glancing up from the electronics book he was reading. "There's no such thing as time travel. *Or* time machines."

I wiped the sweat off my forehead with the back of my sleeve and slouched against the crate. "When have I ever lied to you?" I asked, trying to look hurt and sincere at the same time.

"An interesting question," said Max, carefully laying his book aside on the rumpled cot and holding up his fingers to count on. "Now, let me see. I can recall the Rotten Toboggan Affair . . . "

Uh-oh, here we go. Max has all these code names for the various little misunderstandings we've had. The Rotten Toboggan Affair referred to that day last winter when I talked him into going down Quarter-Mile Hill on a beat-up old toboggan. “You’re crazy,” Max had said. “This hill is too steep and this toboggan is a mess. Look at it. It’s even rotting out underneath.”

It took a lot of doing, but I finally convinced him that the toboggan was as good as new and as sound as a rock. A couple of minutes later, as we were tearing down the hill at about eighty miles an hour, the toboggan began to come apart. Little pieces began breaking off, and we lost control, hit a tree stump, somersaulted through the air, and smashed into a snow bank. Max remembers things like that.

“ . . . and the Taste-Tempting Tip . . . ”

Was it my fault that liver-and-kidney-flavored Puppy Chewies taste worse, not better, than they look?

“ . . . and let’s not forget Operation Lousy Letter!”

See what happens when you try to help a friend? I mean, could I have known that Max, who is always trying to work up the nerve to talk to Dawn Sharington, would get upset when I broke the ice by writing her a love letter and signing his name to it?

“Okay, okay,” I said, holding up my hands in surrender. “Let’s not quibble over a few minor mistakes. After all, what do you care if Dawn knows you think she’s the best-looking girl west of the Mississippi?”

Max made a choking sound.

“Besides, you should thank me. You wanted Dawn to notice you, and now she does. Whenever she sees you, she starts giggling like crazy.”

“Agggggggh,” groaned Max, clutching his head with both hands.

“Look, Max,” I said cheerfully, “forget about the letter. We’ve got something a lot more important to deal with. I mean, haven't we been wondering for the last two weeks what we were going to do all summer? Well, now we've got the answer."

I patted the time-machine crate meaningfully and read the black lettering stamped on the side:

MAINLY, ONE GENUINE, COMPLETELY AUTOMATED, EASILY ASSEMBLED, ONE-OF-A-KIND TIME MACHINE! FULLY GUARANTEED!

"Sure, sure," grumbled Max. "And you got it at a garage sale for two-fifty. You don't expect me to believe that, do you?"

"If you'll just listen a minute," I said, "I can explain the whole thing. Okay?"

Max grunted, but he was still suffering over Dawn. This sales pitch was going to have to be good.

"Okay. You know Mr. Cooper, right? The man who lives just around the corner in that great big old house? Well, he found this crate in his attic last night, and he's sure it was left there by the famous Professor Flybender."

Max's logical mind slowly clicked into gear. "Oh, yeah? If this professor guy is so famous, how come I've lived here in Flat Rock for five years and never heard of him? And why would he leave things in Mr. Cooper's attic?"

"Good points. I asked Mr. Cooper the same things. It turns out that Flybender used to live there and was some sort of crazy inventor. You know, setting off explosions in his basement and racing around on his roof during thunderstorms. About eight years ago, he announced that he was off to find the lost continent of Atlantis, and nobody has seen him since. Eventually, the house was sold to pay off the professor's debts, and Mr. Cooper bought it."

"Okay, Sherlock, then why didn't Mr. Cooper find this marvelous invention before now?" Max smugly pushed his glasses back up on his nose.

"Because, Watson, there was so much junk in the attic when Mr. Cooper bought the house he never had time to go through it all. But this morning he was looking for stuff to put on sale, and that's when he spotted the crate. He dragged it down and put it out with a bunch of chipped dishes and old clothes."

"I still say you've been had," Max insisted stubbornly. "If Mr. Cooper actually believed this was a time machine, do you really think he would have sold it to you?"

"Of course not," I scoffed. I was ready for that one too. "But just because Mr. Cooper is too shortsighted to recognize a great discovery like this doesn't mean we have to be too. After all, you're the one who's always telling me that scientific geniuses are misunderstood in their own times."

Max seemed impressed with this argument, since it was one of his own. Nibbling his thumbnail thoughtfully, he got up and began to circle the crate slowly.

"Well, just for the sake of argument," he said, "let's *suppose* this Professor Flybender really was a brilliant inventor, and *suppose* he really did build this thing, and *suppose* he really did leave it in Mr. Cooper's attic. . . ."

Max's voice trailed off as he mulled over his supposes.

Max is like that. He *thinks* about everything, weighing all the angles, considering all the options. Maybe it comes from being a compulsive reader. I mean, Max goes for books like a hungry piranha goes for toes, which means he knows *something* about almost everything. It also means his brain works overtime. I call him Motor-Mind.

As for me, I prefer action. It saves time. I can eat two ice-cream cones in the time it takes Max to consider the relative merits of vanilla versus peanut-pumpkin swirl.

And I could see it was time to act. I thumped the crate loudly with the flat of my hand—**THUMP.**

"Max, my boy, this is Opportunity Knocking." **THUMP, THUMP.** "Think of it—a *time machine!* A hot rod into history! Why, with this baby we could go anywhere we want—to any *time* we want. Just consider the possibilities!"

THUMP! "We could travel back three thousand years to ancient Egypt and catch the grave robbers as they jimmy their way into King Tut's tomb!"

Max's eyes glazed slightly as he considered that possibility.

THUMP! "We could ride with Attila the Hun and his mighty hordes as they terrorize the Roman Empire!"

"Yeah," whispered Max in an awed voice. "And if we stopped off in the seventeenth century, I could get Shakespeare's autograph!"

He was hooked. Of course, I had no intention of chasing around through time trying to get some guy's autograph, but we could iron out that detail later.

I hopped up onto a stool. "We could drop in on the nineteenth century and solve the Jack the Ripper murders!"

"Wow!" said Max, joining in. "And attend the opening night of Beethoven's Fifth Symphony!"

I jabbed my finger at the ceiling and cried, "Babe Ruth, Billy the Kid, Blackbeard the Pirate!"

"Aristotle, Galileo, Einstein!" Max shouted.

I made a flying leap onto the table, threw back my head, and yelled, "The Gunfight at the O.K. Corral!"

Max was overcome. He snapped to attention and saluted up at me. "Say no more, chief," he said, his face glowing with enthusiasm. "Just tell me what you want me to do."

I jumped down and held out my hand. "Fork over two dollars," I said. "I was a little short of the asking price, and Mr. Cooper said he'd take the time machine back if I didn't come up with the rest of the money before eleven o'clock."

Putting the time machine together was a cinch. We just followed the step-by-step instructions in the professor's booklet on **ASSEMBLING FLYBENDER'S**

FANTASTIC, FULLY GUARANTEED TIME MACHINE. Nobody bothered us either, which is one of the big advantages of having a clubhouse of our own. We'd built it ourselves out in my backyard, where it's almost completely hidden by trees. Even my nosy little sister usually leaves us alone.

By one o'clock, the time machine was finished. As we shook hands and stood back to admire our work, the weird seven-foot-tall contraption seemed to be staring down at us.

"We may have just assembled Flybender's Fantastic Hunk of Junk," commented Max, eyeing the machine doubtfully. "Does this thing look like a time machine to you?"

"You bet," I lied. "And what a beaut."

Actually, Max had a point. It did look sort of like a hunk of junk. In fact, with all the confusion of dials and meters and switches and colored lights, and that ridiculously tiny map of the world pinned under glass, and that enormous **ON-OFF** lever jutting out from the side, the machine could have been anything. Mostly, it looked like a giant jelly-bean dispenser from outer space.

As for the inner workings, they were a complete mystery, because most of the work we'd done was limited to screwing knobs and glass plates and other loose parts onto the outer surface of the machine. Like, for instance, the overgrown fan that, following the professor's instructions, we had bolted on top. I had the uneasy feeling that if we turned that fan on, it would turn the clubhouse inside out.

All in all, it was hard to believe Flybender's machine could transport anybody anywhere—especially through time. But I wasn't going to waste time worrying about it. I believe in positive thinking.

GEORG
TIME
ZONE
Flybender
OPERATING
MANUAL

While I cleaned up, Max fine-tuned the controls, checking the instruction manual to see that the meters were calibrated, the switches were in the correct positions, and all buttons had been pushed in the proper sequence.

I guess you'd say that next to reading, Max's favorite pastime is tinkering with mechanical gadgets. He even put together a pretty impressive robot once, named Big Ed. Last summer we smuggled it up to Camp Wongahana and into a closet in our group's cabin. Then, when all the lights were out, and right in the middle of one of Sid Berman's hair-raising ghost stories, Max pushed a button on his hand-held, remote-control unit, and Big Ed came slamming out of the closet door. His face glowed like a ghoul's, and he made a horrible gurgling noise. Of course, if Sid hadn't been telling ghost stories at the time, everybody probably wouldn't have panicked the way they did, and our counselor wouldn't have led that stampede out of the cabin, screaming, "It's the Un-dead! It's the Un-dead!"

So Max couldn't take *all* the credit for how he and I and Big Ed had the whole cabin to ourselves for the next couple of hours.

Still, he does have a way with machines.

"That's it," said Max, snapping the manual shut. "According to the professor, all we have to do now is select a time and place we want to visit. When our time is up, we'll be automatically returned to the present. And no matter how long we're gone, no time will have passed here, so no one will even know we've been away."

"You mean we'll come back exactly when we left?" I asked.

"That's what the manual says," said Max.

"Great!" I said, pacing the floor with excitement. "And of course since I found the time machine, I get to choose where we go on our first trip. And I choose the Middle Ages."

"The Middle Ages?" said Max, with a puzzled frown. "What's so great about the Middle Ages?"

I slapped my forehead in disgust. "Have you been asleep for the last thirteen years, or what? Haven't you ever heard of knights in shining armor? Haven't you heard of castles and dungeons and damsels in distress? Wouldn't you like a little Action, Adventure, and Excitement?"

"No," said Max.

"I can see it now," I continued, striking a gallant pose. "There we'd be, galloping over the green hills and through the dark forests, rescuing fair maidens who are in danger up to their armpits."

Max snorted. "Everyone knows that all that stuff about rescuing damsels in distress is just a bunch of bunk."

"Oh, yeah? I don't suppose you've ever thought about how it'd be to rescue Dawn Sharington from distress."

Max blushed. "Well," he grumbled, quickly changing the topic, "if we're going to the Middle Ages, we're going to have to nail down the exact date. How does 1250 A.D. sound? That would put us right in the middle of the best century of the whole Middle Ages."

"Whatever you say," I agreed. "You're the history expert."

Max bent toward the control panel of the time machine, squinting. I peered over his shoulder. All the controls were preset except for the three in the center of the panel, outlined with a ring of colored lights. The first was marked "Dial-a-Date." By turning the knobs under the window, you could dial any date you wanted. Max carefully dialed A.D. 1250.

The second control, "Pick-a-Place," had a tiny world map under glass. Max fiddled with the knobs and found that they moved a red dot across the face of the map, marking the place you wanted to be transported to.

"Might as well make it jolly old England," he said, jockeying the red dot into position.

I couldn't believe it—a trip to medieval England! My skin prickled, and I began to beat out a drum roll on the table.

"As for our 'Length-of-Stay,' " continued Max briskly as he examined the third control, "since this is a trial run, I say we drop in for about three hours."

"*Three hours!*" The drums stopped in midroll. "*Three hours!* What can we do in three measly little hours?"

"We can stay out of trouble, that's what." Max squared his shoulders and crossed his arms over his chest. "Take it or leave it. I'm crazy enough just letting you talk me into trying this thing in the first place."

He meant it.

"You win," I sighed.

With a satisfied nod, Max turned to adjust the "Length-of-Stay" controls. He set the numbers knobs to read "003" and then spun the units knob past "Years" and "Days" to lock in on "Hours." Three hours. Big deal. Baseball games can last longer than that.

I was disappointed, and I guess that's why I did it. I know I shouldn't have, but when Max took his glasses off to polish them on his shirttail, I reached over and moved the last numbers knob forward five notches. What could it hurt if we were in the Middle Ages for eight hours instead of three?

To cover myself, I kept an eye on Max and observed loudly, "Do you realize what this means? We're actually going to travel through time! You and me. Steve Brandon and Maximilian Zilinski."

"Yeah." Max's voice wavered, as if he weren't too sure he really liked the idea. "Maybe we should gather up some supplies or sandwiches or something and go tomorrow morning. What do you think?"

I hate waiting. Besides, waiting might give Max time to change his mind.

"There's no time like the present," I said.

"Then why are we going to the Middle Ages?" said Max dryly.

He put his glasses back on and started for the door. "Anyway," he added, "why don't we go over to my house and have something to eat? My mother can make us one of her famous avocado-and-chili sandwiches, and we can talk the whole thing over."

I figured it was now or never.

Almost without thinking, I reached out, grasped the huge **ON-OFF** lever, and by throwing my full weight against it, pulled it down to "**ON**." Max spun around, but

there was nothing he could do. He was clear across the room, with his hand on the doorknob and one foot out the door. I barely had time to glimpse his startled expression before Professor Flybender's Fully Guaranteed Time Machine sprang to life.

Lights flashed, gauges gyrated, steam spewed out of loose joints with the force of a fire hose turned on full blast.

Flybender's machine was working, all right.

Then, from deep inside, came a weird, wild, wailing sound. It was low like a moan but rose steadily until it reached an eerie high pitch. And at that moment the giant fan on top of the machine began to spin, ghostly slow at first, but gaining speed . . . faster . . . faster. . . .

The clubhouse began to vibrate . . . faster. . . . I was thrown up hard against the shaking walls . . . faster. . . . Max began to look fuzzy around the edges . . . faster. . . . Now he was a blur . . . faster. . . .

"Max!" I shouted. And was immediately plunged into darkness.

The wind whistled by in furious whirlwinds, howling around my head and pulling at my hair. I felt as if I were on a vibrating conveyor belt, out of control and hurtling through a long ink-black tunnel.

A panicky feeling welled up inside me. I pushed it down and tried to call out to Max, but the wind caught his name and swept it away.

Where was Max? Why was this taking so long? Why weren't we in the Middle Ages? Why—

Without warning, the vibrating stopped, and I fell several feet, landing with a heavy thud.

It was all over, but where was I? There were no lights, no sounds.

Blinking into the blackness, I tried to look around, but for some reason I couldn't move my neck. I tried to stand up but discovered that I couldn't move my legs. I tried a dog paddle, but it was no go. *I was pinned.*

Now what? I wondered grimly.

Suddenly, I was startled by a strange, clinky-jingling noise and the uncomfortable feeling that I was turning, like a chicken on a barbecue spit, slowl-l-l-l-ly in space.

A narrow slit of light appeared in front of my eyes.

Then, into that slit of light popped a face—round, eager, about sixteen years old, with brown bobbed hair. He examined me with concern for a few moments before asking anxiously, "Art thou all right, Sir Robert?"

Before I could answer, the round-faced stranger pulled me to a sitting position and lifted a massive, flat-topped helmet off my head. I gaped down at myself in amazement.

No wonder I made a clinking noise whenever I moved. My T-shirt, jeans, and tennis shoes were gone. In their place was a long chain-mail shirt that covered me from head to knee, and underneath that, a pair of chain-mail tights. Over the armor, I was sporting a sleeveless, emerald-green tunic with a coat of arms embroidered in gold across my chest. And from my belt hung a long sword in a gold scabbard.

But even more amazing, I was wearing *someone else's body!* Someone tall and broad-shouldered, with plenty of well-developed muscles.

Not bad, I thought to myself, as I flexed my arm and felt the muscles ripple.

"Art thou all right, Sir Robert?" repeated the stranger. He was wearing a simple brown tunic over green tights, and soft leather boots with pointed toes.

"I sure art," I said cheerfully. As I spoke, I noticed that even my voice was different. It was deeper than my own, and stronger too. "But if you don't mind my asking, who art you?"

"Why, I am Niles, Sir Robert. Thy squire. Dost thou not know me?" He shook his head and looked worried. "Thou hast taken a nasty tumble off thy horse, and methinks it hath rattled thy wits."

He was wrong there. My wits were in tip-top condition. In fact, you might say that my wits were doing handsprings for joy as I realized several things:

- Flybender's machine had worked after all, and I was in the Middle Ages as planned.
- I had been transported into the body of a Sir Robert, a knight, and this guy, Niles, was his squire.
- As I entered Sir Robert's body, I must have gotten dizzy and fallen off my horse, which explained why Niles thought my wits were rattled, and why I had arrived with my nose in the dirt.

Then it hit me. If I came back in someone else's body, Max could be here, too, and I'd never recognize him. I began to look around with serious interest.

I was on a grassy field, surrounded by a makeshift camp of large, brightly colored tents, each decorated with flags and pennants that fluttered in the breeze. Looming a short distance to the right were the gray stone walls and turrets of a medieval castle. And by my side stood a sleek white horse draped with yards and yards of green cloth trimmed in gold.

Here and there men and boys scurried, all dressed like Niles in tunics and tights. Max could be anywhere, even miles from here.

I realized that if I were ever going to find him, I'd need a lot more information. And as Niles helped me to my feet, I thought of a plan to get it.

I shook my head as if I were still dazed. "Niles," I said, hoping I looked lost and confused, "I can't seem to get my bearings. I'm afraid that falling off my horse has made me lose my memory. Maybe if you'd tell me where we are and what we're doing here, it will all come back to me."

It worked. Niles looked up at me anxiously, with loyal devotion written all over his face. "Why, Sir Robert, we are at the Great Hampshire Tournament, where we have camped these past three days in thy tent." He gestured to the yellow-gold tent with green banners that stood behind us. "We came at the invitation of Richard Lorraine, Earl of Hampshire, who heard tales of thy great strength and skill at jousting and would try thee against his own champion. 'Tis the last day of the tourney, and thou art undefeated as usual, sire. Eighteen knights have fallen already before thy lance. There remaineth only the joust with Sir Bevis, a minor feat for someone with thy mighty talents."

I nodded cautiously. "I see. And just when is this minor jousting match supposed to take place?"

"In but a few moments, Sir Robert," he said, busily dusting off my tunic and straightening my belt. "Then the tourney will be over, and thou wilt be the champion. The people await this last joust most eagerly."

"Hmmmm. And you think I can handle Sir Bevis, do you?"

Niles laughed merrily. "Oh, Sir Robert, thou art jesting, of course. 'Twill be a sad day for English knighthood when thou, the Green Falcon, canst not best the likes of Sir Bevis."

Bingo! Jackpot! Things were looking good. Not only was I in the Middle Ages, but I was in the body of a famous knight and was actually going to be in a jousting match on the field of honor! And it was my kind of contest—me against some harmless, lily-livered, mealy-mouthed twerp.

The only problem was that it all sounded a bit beneath my talents. Why then, I wondered, were the people so eager to see this particular match? I decided to fish for a few details.

"Tell me, Niles," I said, cracking my knuckles and flexing my muscles, "who is this Bevis turkey anyway?"

"Why, Sir Bevis Thorkell," replied Niles cheerfully, "the Earl's champion and a knight known throughout all England as the Hampshire Mauler."

"The Hampshire *Mauler*?" I didn't like the sound of that.

"Aye, Sir Robert, and a black-hearted varlet he is. Canst thou truly remember nothing? Dost thou not recall his vow to smash thy skull and feed thy guts to the castle dogs, the saucy fellow ?"

Saucy fellow? This was his idea of a saucy fellow? Something began to tell me I might not be cut out for the field of honor after all.

Niles continued gleefully. "Ho, ho! But I did put Sir Bevis in his place. Not two hours ago I met the knave within the castle walls. 'Is thy master ready to meet his doom?' he did ask me. 'Best thou lookest to thine own health,' I replied. 'Sir Robert will this very afternoon whack thee from thy horse, pommel and pound thee, and smite thee to smithereens.' "

"Gee," I said, laughing nervously. "I hope he didn't take that the wrong way."

Niles nodded happily. "That blow to thy head hath not robbed thee of thy sense of humor, Sir Robert." He chuckled contentedly to himself.

I found myself wondering if Sir Bevis and I could talk this thing over. I mean, I didn't want to be a spoilsport or anything, but let's face it, I don't perform well under pressure.

"Niles," I said, looking for an out, "give it to me straight. What has Sir Bevis got against me?"

" 'Tis no secret, sire. Sir Bevis is sore jealous that thou art a knight and are but eighteen years of age. He himself was not knighted until his twenty-first year, as is the common custom. And 'tis well-known that the Earl hath taken a liking to thee during the tournament. Mayhap Sir Bevis feareth that thou wilt replace him as the Earl's champion."

Niles blushed slightly. "And, of course, there is the matter of Lady Elizabeth."

"Oh?" I asked suspiciously. "What matter would that be?"

Niles's blush deepened and he looked away, embarrassed. "Ah, well, since thou hast lost thy memory, Sir Robert, I suppose I must admit that even I have noticed the glances that have passed between thyself and the Earl's fair daughter. And since Sir Bevis hopeth to make the Lady his wife, this hath only angered him the more."

"Okay," I said, shifting my weight uneasily. "Let me get this straight. Sir Bevis is a little upset because he thinks I'm trying to steal his reputation, his job, and his girl. Right?"

"Aye. And thou art just the man to do it."

"But—"

Suddenly, there was a loud blast of trumpets from somewhere nearby.

"Make haste, sire!" gasped Niles. " 'Tis time!"

Before I could say another word, he clapped the iron helmet back onto my head. A page ran out of a nearby tent, carrying some portable stairs which he plunked down next to the white stallion. I was still confused and stunned as Niles hustled me up the stairs and onto the horse, thrusting a shield into my left hand and a ten-foot-long lance into my right.

With a hearty "Go to, Sir Robert!" he slapped the horse's backside, and off we trotted in the direction of the trumpets.

"Where is Max now that I need him?" I groaned.

"Right here," said a deep voice from under me. "And you have my full support!"

It was Max! He was my horse!

"I heard everything Niles said," he continued with a whinny, "and I think it's safe to say that we're about to experience a little Action, Adventure, and Excitement."

With that, Max snorted noisily and pranced out onto the field of honor, proudly tossing his mane and humming the Notre Dame fight song, while I struggled wildly to hold my lance upright and stay in the saddle.

Lining one side of the large open field were long wooden bleachers crowded with cheering spectators. Women waved their scarves and handkerchiefs. Men stood and shouted. From the tops of tall poles, colored banners streamed and flapped in the breeze. On a raised platform behind the bleachers, twenty heralds snapped to attention, pressed golden trumpets to their lips, and blared out a rousing call to arms.

Little League was never like this.

Max tossed his head toward a lone figure mounted on a black steed at the opposite end of the field. "That must be Sir Bevis," he neighed.

It was the Hampshire Mauler, all right, and he looked ready to maul anything that got in his way. His chain mail, shield, sword, and helmet were coal black; and a blood-red tunic dripped from his massive shoulders. Even from a distance, he looked like a killer. I swallowed hard.

"Uh, look, Max," I stammered, "don't you think we should make a break for it before somebody around here gets hurt?"

"Relax," said Max, pawing the dirt eagerly. "I happen to know for a fact that jousting is more or less the safest of all the deadly dangerous sports in medieval England."

"Terrific," I said. "How silly of me to worry. I mean, what do I care about a ten-foot-long lance in the gut?"

Before Max could answer, the heralds blasted forth with another jarring fanfare. A hush fell over the crowd, and almost as a single body, they leaned forward in their seats. My heart took a nose dive down into where my tennis shoes should have been.

"Now what?" I hissed.

"No problem," whispered Max. "All you have to do is watch Sir Bevis and do whatever he does."

"Oh, sure," I said. "That's just great. And what if he runs me through with his lance?"

"In that case," said Max, "try not to land on your head. It'll only make matters worse."

I would have let him have it with my spurs, but I didn't have time. I caught some movement out of the corner of my eye, and I looked down the long field through the slits in my helmet. In the center were two narrow lanes separated by a low fence. And at the far end was Sir Bevis—evil, threatening, poised for the kill.

He lowered his lance until it was level and aimed steadily across the field straight at my heart.

What else could I do? I lowered my lance. It wobbled around like crazy.

Abruptly, the trumpets stopped, leaving the shock of silence. In that same instant, Sir Bevis spurred his black

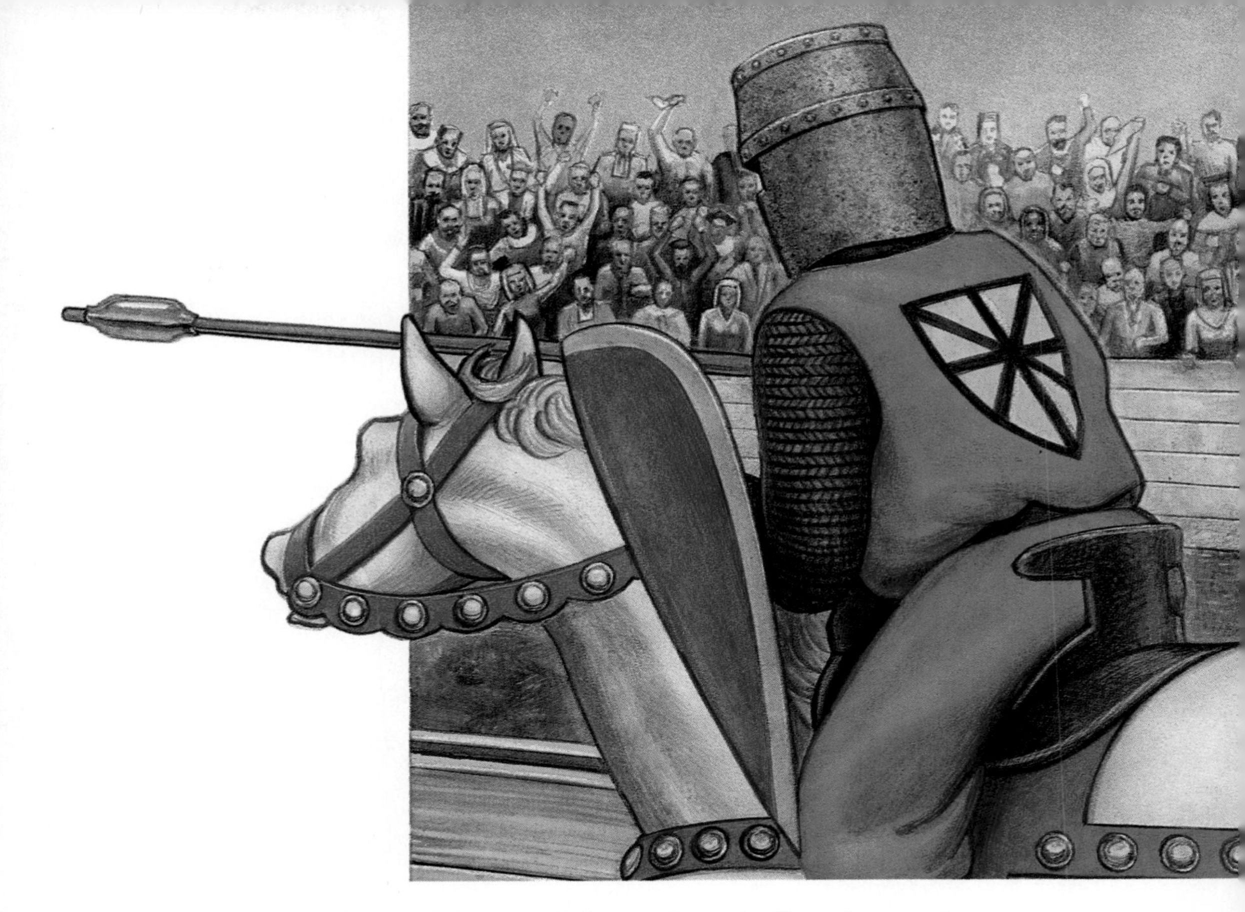

stallion and charged forward, his red tunic flapping and the tip of his lance glinting in the sun.

Without a word, Max too leaped forward. We were on a collision course with the Hampshire Mauler.

The muffled thunder of hoofbeats filled the air. Hypnotized, I locked my eyes on the black figure bearing down on us. A cold fear gripped my spine, and I tried desperately to steady my lance.

He was almost upon us—so close that I thought I glimpsed his wild eyes gleaming evilly behind the slits in his black helmet. I braced myself for a terrible blow.

Suddenly, just before I was due to swallow the tip of Sir Bevis's lance, Max opened his mouth, curled back his lips, and at the top of his lungs bellowed: **"GERONIMO-O-O-O-O-O-O-O-O-O!"**

Sir Bevis's horse gave an alarmed squeal, dug all four hooves into the ground, and skidded to an abrupt halt.

Sir Bevis catapulted out of the saddle, sailed through the air, and fell with a noisy **CLANK!** onto the field. He was knocked out cold.

Child's play, I thought to myself as Max slowed to a stop and turned around. *This jousting business is mere child's play.*

The crowd went wild. And so they should. It was a brilliant performance.

Of course, from the bleachers, no one heard Max yell or saw that I had never laid a lance on Sir Bevis. All they knew was that on the very first pass, the Hampshire Mauler had been easily unhorsed and lay in a dazed heap on the field. And I was not about to spoil their fun by setting the record straight.

After all, it was the least I could do for Sir Robert while I was occupying his body. Being a hero, I mean.

Keeping up the old boy's image in his absence. I'd do the same for anyone.

Max must have felt the same way, because he took plenty of time prancing past the stands, swishing his tail all over the place and snorting fiercely like some kind of wild Arabian stallion.

In the center of the stands was a special section covered with a fringed canopy. As we got closer, I could make out a stern-looking man with a rugged, sun-weathered face sitting under the canopy in a thronelike chair. Beside him was a strikingly pretty girl of about sixteen. She was blushing up a storm and had her eyes cast down at her lap, where she was twisting a long white scarf. Standing beside her, bobbing around gleefully, was a scrawny, gray-haired old woman, who waved us forward like a ground crewman bringing in a jumbo jet. She pointed a bony finger at the girl and winked at me.

Max whispered up at me out of the corner of his mouth. "That man is probably our host, the Earl of Hampshire. And you're in luck, Steve. That girl must be Lady Elizabeth."

"What do you mean, I'm in luck?" I hissed back.

Max didn't answer. Instead, he pulled up in front of the fringed box and, without any warning, bent his front legs and *bowed* before the Earl! The spectators gasped and applauded even more loudly. From everywhere came cries of "Sir Robert! Sir Robert! The Green Falcon!" Flowers flew through the air and fell at our feet. I guess they'd never seen a kneeling horse before.

Unfortunately, I had never been *on* a kneeling horse before. I was caught by surprise and was almost pitched out of the saddle. My lance swung down into the box,

nearly nicking the Earl on the nose. He sat back cross-eyed with a startled grunt.

While I struggled to recover, Lady Elizabeth sprang forward and, with lightning speed, tied her white scarf onto the tip of my lance before I could regain my balance and pull it away. Then she fell back into her seat, smiling at me shyly and fluttering her eyelashes. I was glad I was still inside my helmet.

As Max stood up again, Niles suddenly appeared at our side, leading Sir Bevis's black stallion and carrying his black sword. I had read enough about the Middle Ages to know that when a knight wins a jousting match, he wins the other knight's armor and horse, although the loser usually buys back the loot. I guessed that Niles had taken Sir Bevis's sword and horse as a sort of token, since it wouldn't have been polite to strip him of his full armor while he was out cold on the field.

Niles put the sword down and untied Lady Elizabeth's scarf from my lance.

"Ahhhh," he exclaimed in a low voice, " 'twas a gesture of true love." Then, while my hands were full and I couldn't defend myself, he reached up and tucked the scarf inside my tunic—next to my heart. Lady Elizabeth giggled. The old woman skipped from foot to foot, chortling and rubbing her hands together with glee.

I was beginning to wish that Sir Bevis *had* run me through with his lance.

person's health, personality, and future are determined by the stars.

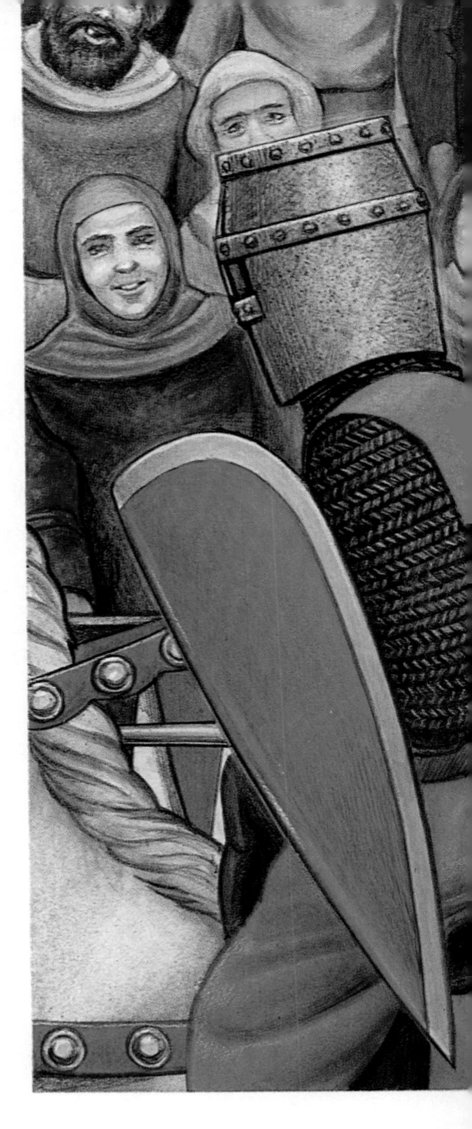

The Earl stood up to make a speech. He threw off his fur-lined cloak and stepped forward, holding up his hand as a signal for silence. The cheers died slowly away.

"Sir Robert Marshall," he boomed for all to hear, "never before have we seen such skill at arms as thou hast shown these past three days. Henceforth, let it be known throughout the land that thou wert the undefeated champion of the Hampshire Tournament in the year of our Lord, twelve hundred and fifty!"

Then, stroking his mustache, he added, "I would count it an honor, Sir Robert, if thou wouldst tarry a while as a guest here at Hampshire Castle. What sayest thou?"

Figuring that Sir Robert would want to accept, I cleared my throat and said, "I'd be happy to, your Earlship."

"Good, good," said the Earl. "Then thou wilt surely join us on the morrow for the hunt. We meet at dawn in the outer bailey."

Without waiting for a reply, he eased himself back into his chair, and the crowd immediately broke into a new storm of cheers and applause. So, while Niles led Sir Bevis's horse back to our tent, Max and I finished parading in front of the stands.

Even when we finally turned and headed back across the field, the thunder of applause followed us. It was great, but I felt a little sad when I realized that within a few short hours we'd be leaving the Middle Ages and winging our way back to our own time. We'd be trading tournaments for TV. It'd be good-bye to glory and hello to hanging around. I heaved a long sigh.

Max, on the other hand, was in high spirits.

"Hey, how about that Geronimo Gimmick?" he whinnied cheerfully. "Pretty terrific, don't you think? And I thought of it *joust* in time." He tittered at his own joke.

"Yeah," I sighed. "Terrific."

"But the best part was that Sir Bevis fell for it. Get it? *Fell* for it!"

"Oh, brother," I muttered, as Max gave a horsy guffaw and trotted briskly across the field toward Sir Robert's tent.

THINKING ABOUT IT

1. You get to use Professor Flybender's time machine. What will the time and destination be, and why?

2. If Steve had not known the dial of the time machine was set for A.D. 1250, he could still have figured out where he was when he landed. What clues told him, and you, that he was in England during the Middle Ages?

3. You are invited by Steve and Max to travel with them to the Middle Ages. You may bring one item from your room to keep during your stay. What is it? How will it help the three of you survive?

Another Book About Medieval Times

Exploring the Past: The Middle Ages, by Catherine Oakes, uses words and many pictures to show what life was like for rulers, lords, knights, and common people in medieval Europe.

Journey to Technos

from *Plays Magazine*

BY Claire Boiko

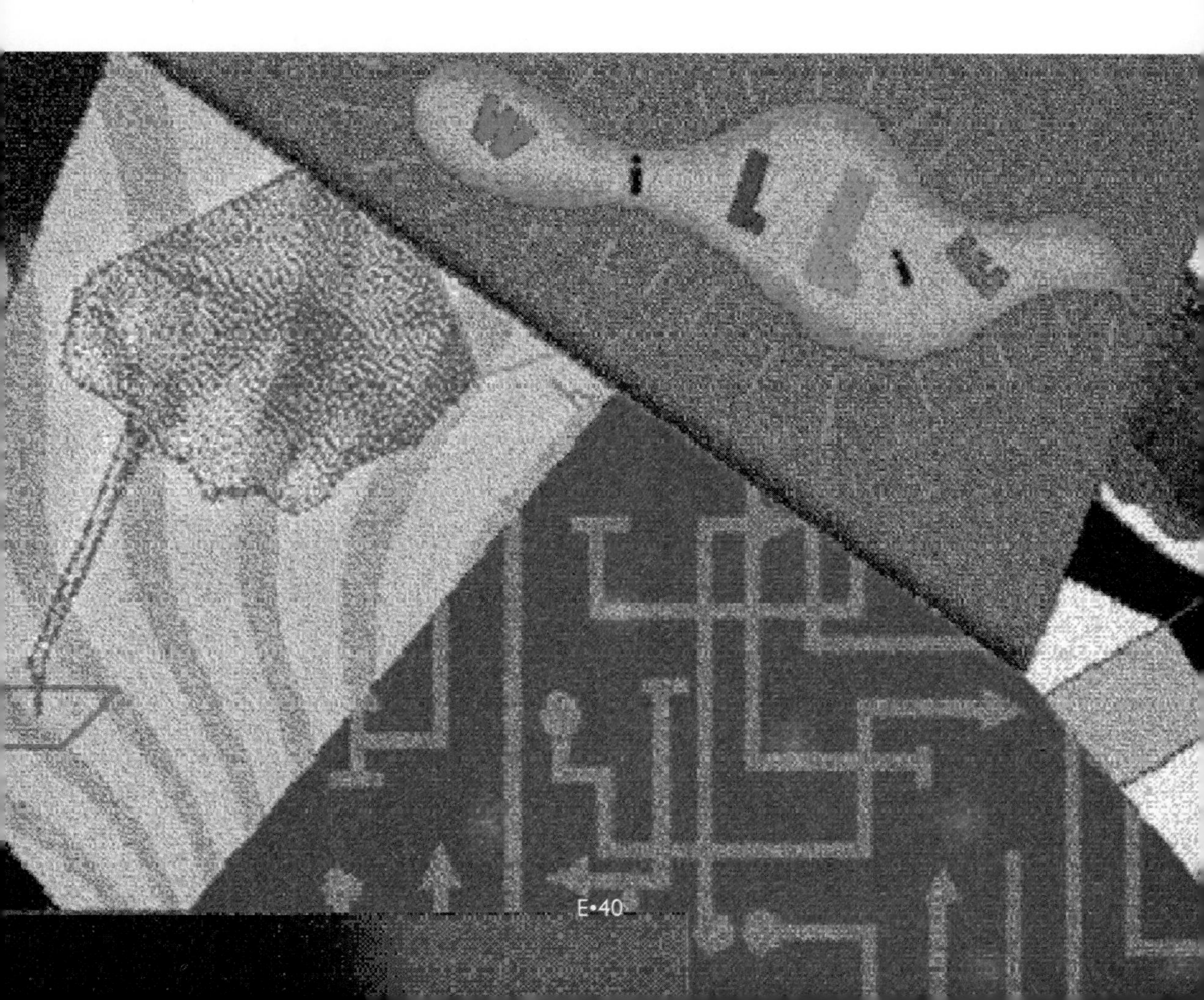

TIME: **PRESENT**

Characters

Willie	Supreme Technocrat
Willie's Mother	**Bits,** *4 or more*
Ginny	BYTES, *4 or more*
Mike	Commanders, *4 or more*
Shannon	Recorded Voices
Peter	

SETTING *A basement workshop. Upstage is a cinder-block wall with uncurtained windows. There is a worktable up center, holding broken television sets, computers, radios, electronic junk, and tools. Hanging above the table is a single shaded light. At right is a dilapidated bookshelf with technical manuals, coils of wire, and tool sets. Scattered left and right are boxes and cartons. Down right is a door leading to the outside, with posters reading,* DANGER, HIGH VOLTAGE! GIANT BRAIN AT WORK. *On upstage wall is a large sign reading,* REPAIRS AT REASONABLE PRICES. YOU BRING IT—I FIX IT. W. WURTZBURGER. *Down left are stairs leading to rest of house.*

Scene 1

AT RISE *Willie Wurtzburger sits on high stool at worktable, absorbed in repairing the inside of a computer.*

Mother *(Calling from off left):* Willie! Willie! Are you down there?

Willie *(Calling off):* Yes, Mom! *(*MOTHER *enters carrying a bulky package.)*

Mother: I have a package for you. It must be important. It came Special Delivery. *(She sets package on worktable.)*

Willie *(Casually):* Oh. Thanks, Mom.

Mother: Aren't you going to open it?

Willie: No hurry. It's some technical stuff I ordered. A randiform magnum circuit with a bilocated flabongo.

Mother *(Nervously):* It won't explode, will it? Remember, you burned out all the fuses last week.

Willie *(Holding up hand; solemnly):* I promise. No explosions.

Mother: I certainly hope not. Now, dear, you will get some fresh air this afternoon, won't you?

Willie *(Distractedly):* Sure, Mom. Don't worry. *(She exits. As soon as she is gone, he dives for box, unwrapping it quickly, speaking to* *himself.)* It's here! That was fast. I ordered it only three days ago. *(Removes a laser-like device from box and holds it at arm's length)* Wow-ee! *(Reads from tag attached to the device)* "Congratulations! You are the owner of A Model One Experimental Probability Wave Amplifier. Now you can explore millions of parallel universes." Fantastic! *(Knocking is heard at door, right.* WILLIE *shoves amplifier back into box and stands in front of it.)* Come in. The door's open. *(*GINNY *enters down right, a letter in her hand.)*

GINNY: Hi, Willie. Has the vice-president of the Science Club got a minute for the president?

Willie: Sure, Madam President. What's happening?

Ginny: A minor glitch in our arrangements. The Science Club was supposed to meet at my house tonight, but my mother's aerobics class is going to take over the rec room, so—

Willie: I'm way ahead of you, Ginny. The club can meet here tonight. What's on the agenda?

Ginny *(Waving letter):* This crazy letter. Listen to this: *(Reading aloud)* "Dear Future Scientist. The Techno Company is offering you an experimental probability wave amplifier. Be the first in your neighborhood to explore new worlds. Experience the thrill of a lifetime free of charge and without obligation of any kind. Offer is limited." *(Looks up)* Can you believe the nerve of the Techno Company? What a fake.

Willie: I got the same letter. *(Uneasily)* How can you be so sure it's a fake?

Ginny: Because it's free. My father says nothing in this world is free. He thinks we should report this whole business to the Better Business Bureau.

Willie *(Crossing to stand so that his back is hiding the box on the worktable again):* Don't you think that's going a little too far?

Ginny: No. The other members of the Science Club probably got letters too. We have to protect them, Willie. *(She rises, crossing right of* WILLIE, *waving letter.)* This is our responsibility. *(Notices box, looks into it, discovers amplifier)* What on earth is this thing? *(Puts letter on table, points to amplifier)*

Willie: Oh, that thing. *(Lamely)* That's a—a—hair dryer.

Ginny *(Reading from tag):* "Congratulations. You are the owner of A Model One Experimental Probability Wave Amplifier."—Willie! I don't believe you fell for that phony advertisement.

Willie: You don't have to tell the whole world, Ginny. Besides—I only ordered it to—um—expose it for the worthless piece of junk it probably is.

Ginny *(Wisely):* Sure, Willie. OK. You're the expert. Show me how it's supposed to work.

Willie *(Reading tag):* "To visit an alternate world, set the blue phase dial at maximum . . . ." *(Sets dial)* "Maximum" it is. That's funny. The advertisement says you can visit millions of alternate universes . But look at this—there's a setting for only one universe.

Ginny: Bad engineering. Just what you'd expect from a phony operation like this.

Willie: I guess so. What's next? *(Reading)* "Turn the switch, place yourself in front of the amplifier, and prepare for the thrill of a lifetime—" *(*GINNY *stands center, in front of amplifier.)* Are you ready for the thrill of a lifetime?

Ginny: I can't wait. Beam me up, Scotty.

Willie: Here goes the switch. *(Flips switch. Siren wails. Blackout. Thunderclap.* GINNY *exits. Lights up full. Amplifier spotlight remains center.* WILLIE, *bewildered, runs left and right searching for* GINNY.*)* Ginny? Hey, Ginny. Very funny. Come out, come out, wherever you are.

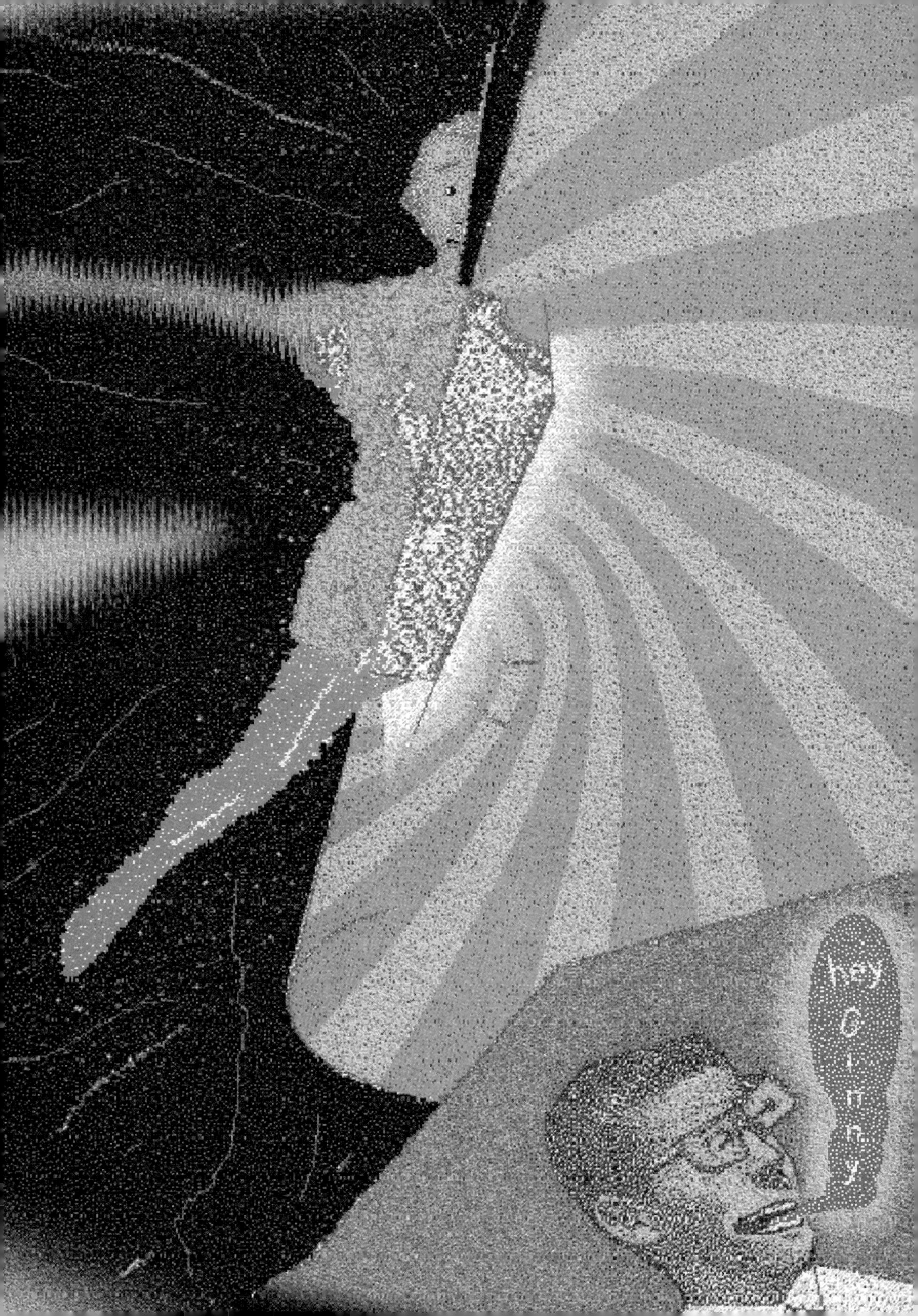
hey Ginny

Ginny *(Offstage, wailing):* Help! Help me, Willie!

Willie *(Crossing to center spotlight circle, dropping to hands and knees, frantically patting the circle):* Are you in there? Answer me, Ginny. What happened? *(He stands in circle of light, reaching up, feeling the air.)* Where are you? *(Frantic)* She's vanished—into thin air. *(Points angrily at amplifier)* And it's all your fault! *(Siren, blackout, thunderclap, as before.* WILLIE *exits.)*

Willie *(Offstage):* Hey, what's happening? Where am I? *(Voice fades off.)* O-h-h-h! *(Lights up full. Spotlight circle center goes on.* MOTHER *enters on stairs, left.)*

Mother: Willie, did you call me? That's odd. I could have sworn he called me. *(Crossing center, looking around)* That's good. He went out for a breath of fresh air after all! *(Crosses to amplifier, turns it off. Spotlight goes off.)* Oh, Willie, you're so careless with your equipment! *(She exits, left. Blackout. Curtain. Synthesizer music is played.)*

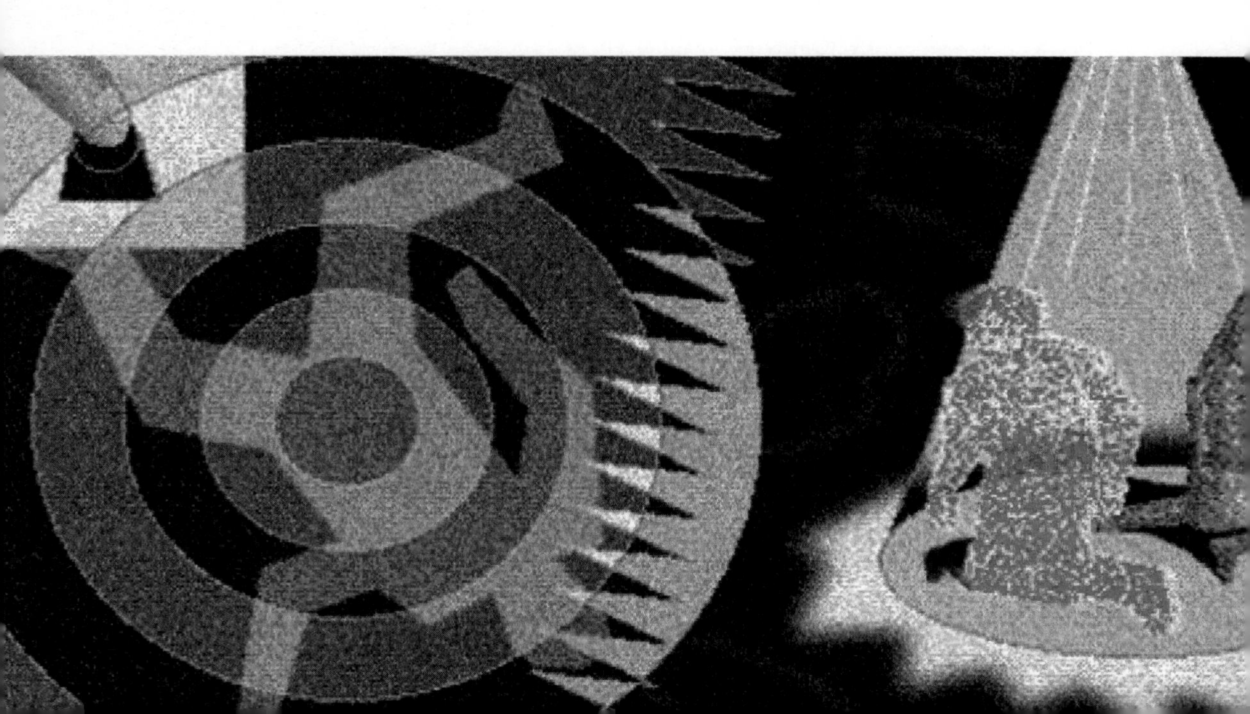

Scene 2

BEFORE RISE *Stage is dark. Music stops. Siren, then thunderclap.* GINNY *enters, illuminated by spotlight, down right.*

Ginny *(Frantically):* Doesn't anybody hear me? Help! *(Siren, thunderclap, blackout, as* WILLIE *enters down right, in spotlight with* GINNY. GINNY *grabs him, relieved.)* Willie, I'm so glad you're here. *(Scared)* Willie, where are we?

Willie: I don't know.

1st Recorded Voice: Welcome to Technos, Travelers.

Willie: Who—who's there?

Ginny: Where are you?

1st Recorded Voice: Have no fear, Travelers. The darkness and disorientation are temporary inconveniences. You are in a buffer zone between your universe and the universe of Technos, the All-Perfect Society.

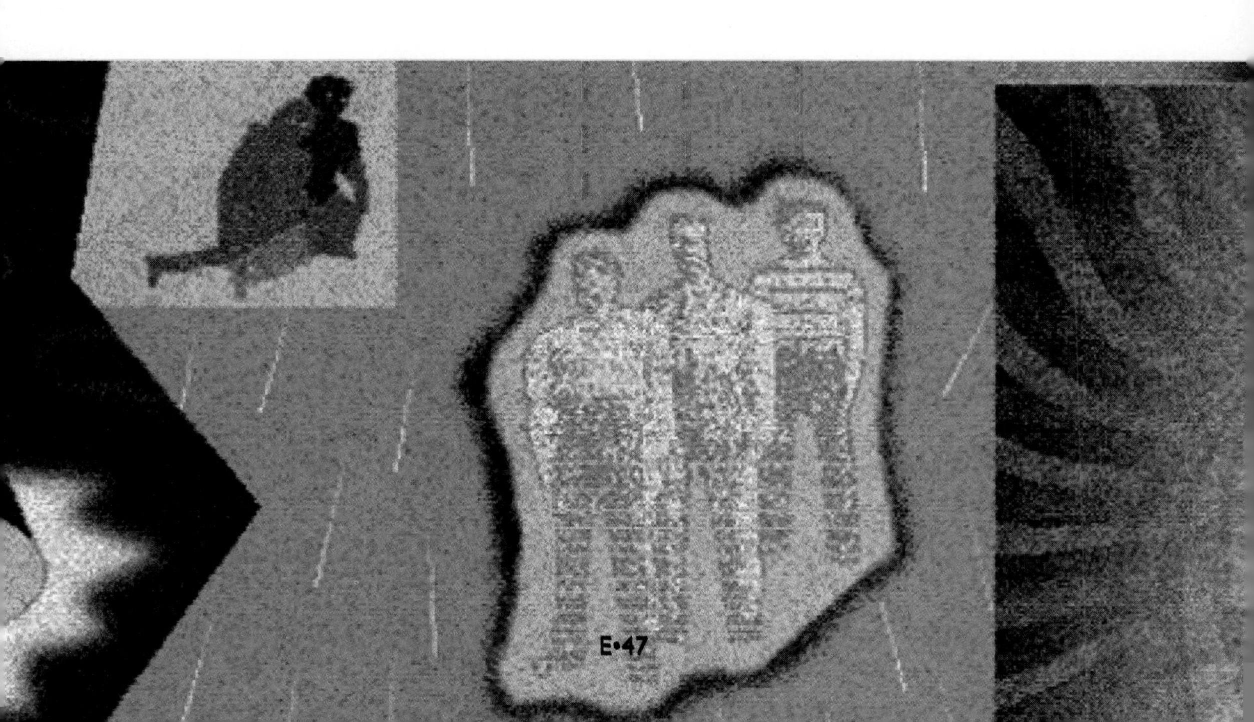

Ginny: Another universe? Oh, Willie, this is incredible!

Willie: What do you think it all means, Ginny?

Ginny *(Wailing):* I wish you hadn't answered that letter.

1st Recorded Voice: Please wait on your lighted entrance circle until the other Travelers arrive.

Ginny: What other Travelers?

Willie *(Grimly):* Other suckers who ordered the Probability Wave Amplifier, of course.

Ginny: Willie, something's terribly wrong here.

Willie: You're telling me. Listen, Ginny, I think we ought to keep as low a profile as possible in this universe. When those other Travelers arrive, we're going to duck out of this—*(Pointing down at spotlight circle)* this "entrance circle" and play it cool until we know what's really going on.

Ginny: I'm with you. The more we know, the better. *(Siren, blackout, and thunderclap. First spotlight circle remains onstage throughout the following scene.)*

Willie *(Grabbing* GINNY'S *hand and pulling her down right, urgently):* Now, Ginny! *(They crouch beside spotlight circle, watching as second spotlight comes up on* MIKE, SHANNON, *and* PETER. *As* WILLIE *starts to call out to them,* GINNY *puts her hand over his mouth.)*

Ginny: Shh! We're keeping a low profile, remember?

Willie: But it's Mike, Shannon, and Peter, the rest of the Science Club.

Ginny: I know, but I have a strong hunch that we'd better keep still.

Mike, Shannon, & Peter *(Ad lib):* Help! Somebody, help us!

2nd Recorded Voice: Welcome to Technos, Travelers. You are the first voyagers to arrive in our universe. *(*MIKE, SHANNON, *and* PETER *huddle together, terrified.)*

Mike: Technos? We're in some weird universe called Technos? Man, I wish we'd never ordered those amplifiers.

Shannon: How do we get out of here?

2nd Recorded Voice: You are honored guests. You will be provided with a lighted walkway and several Information Bits for your comfort and safety. *(A strip of green and white blinking lights comes on—outlines the outer rim of the apron.* THREE INFORMATION BITS, *in blue trousers, tunics with binary number 1, enter left, right, and center surrounding* MIKE, SHANNON, *and* PETER. *They bow in unison.)*

Bits *(In unison):* Greetings, in the name of the Supreme Technocrat! We are your Primary Information Bits. We will accompany you to the city of Technos.

Shannon *(Aside):* This is getting weirder and weirder. *(To* BITS*)* We can't go with you. We never go places with strangers.

1st Bit: You must come with us.

Mike: No, you don't understand. We want to go home.

Peter *(Confidentially to* BITS*):* Now, listen, you guys. We appreciate all this hospitality. You shouldn't have gone to all the trouble, because honestly, we can't stay another minute. We all have tons of homework, and an important Science Club meeting tonight. You understand, don't you? Just point us toward Earth—we'll do the rest.

2nd Bit: You refuse to accompany us? We must summon the Commanders. *(Holds out beeper, which sounds an alarm.* Three COMMANDERS, *in red helmets, red trousers, tunics with lightning slashes across front, enter on the run, left, right, and through curtain, center. Their index fingers are capped with long silver points.)*

Commanders *(Together):* What is the problem?

Bits *(Together):* Noncompliance.

Commanders *(To* MIKE, SHANNON, *and* PETER*):* You will obey us, or suffer the consequences.

Shannon: Never. Remember the Maine.

Mike: Remember the Alamo.

Peter: Remember the Science Club! *(They cheer.)*

1st Commander: If you will not come as guests, then you must come as prisoners. *(*COMMANDERS *surround the spotlighted circle as* BITS *move back respectfully.* COMMANDERS *aim pointed index fingers at Science Club members. As they do so, lights flicker. There is a buzzing sound.)* Come this way. *(They point off left.* MIKE, SHANNON, *and* PETER *sway dizzily, then stiffen like zombies.* COMMANDERS *point upward. All form a line, a* COMMANDER *at the head,* MIKE, SHANNON, *and* PETER *in the middle, two* COMMANDERS *and* BITS *following.)*

2nd Commander: The Supreme Technocrat will be pleased. We have brought him fresh minds for his Memory Core. *(All raise arms in salute.)* Hail, Supreme Technocrat!

Bits: Hail, Supreme Technocrat! *(They march off left.* WILLIE *and* GINNY *cross center, apprehensively.)*

Ginny: Brainwashed! *(Snaps fingers)* Just like that. Willie, this is scary. What do we do now?

Willie: Follow them. Come on! *(They run off left. Bridge of synthesizer music is heard. Spotlights and strip lights go off.)*

Scene 3

SETTING *Outdoor court of* SUPREME TECHNOCRAT. *Backdrop shows giant computer memory core. In front, center, is large silver throne. Flanking the throne are two* COMMANDERS, *at attention. Left and right of backdrop are bare, metallic trees. At left is a counter holding blue tunics. At right is a counter holding pitcher and small paper cups. Down left and right are low metallic walls set at an angle so that they do not hide action.*

AT RISE WILLIE *pokes his head out from behind curtain, down left, then beckons to* GINNY, *who is behind him. They crawl cautiously on, hiding behind low wall.*

Willie: I don't see the others, do you?

Ginny *(Shaking head):* No. *(Shudders)* What a creepy place. *(Points to backdrop)* Look at the size of that memory core. You could store information from a million encyclopedias in that thing.

3rd Recorded Voice: Attention. Attention. *(*WILLIE *and* GINNY *crouch lower.)* Vendor Bytes, please report to your stations. . . .*(*VENDOR BYTES, *wearing yellow trousers, tunics with binary number 8, and yellow caps, enter up left and right. They cross behind counters.)*

4th Recorded Voice: Attention. Attention. All Information Bits report to Vendor Bytes for clean tunics and nutriments. *(*INFORMATION BITS, *wearing blue T-shirts, enter up left and line up at tunic counter.* BITS *entering from right wear tunics, line up at* RIGHT VENDOR.)

Left Vendor: Bits, don your tunics! *(*BITS *put on tunics.* WILLIE *motions to* GINNY, *and they cross to tunic counter, put on tunics.)*

SUPREME TECHNOCRAT: You have done well. Summon the new minds. I am hungry for the information they contain. *(*COMMANDERS *point off left. Zapping sound; lights flicker.* MIKE, SHANNON, *and* PETER *enter single file, like sleepwalkers; they wear metallic helmets.* COMMANDERS *point to a spot in front of* SUPREME TECHNOCRAT. *The three kneel before* TECHNOCRAT, *who raises his hands slowly above their heads.)*

All *(Except* WILLIE *and* GINNY*):* A-h-h-h . . . ! *(* WILLIE *motions* GINNY *to sneak down right, behind wall.)*

Ginny: What are we going to do? That monster is going to steal the brains of the three smartest kids in the state!

Willie: I was hoping you'd have some answers.

Ginny: I'm pretty sure those local yokels aren't robots. They have to be fed, and robots don't eat.

Willie: So they're human. Brainwashed or hypnotized, but human. So what do we do?

Ginny: We do something to break up all that "togetherness." Make those zombies behave like individuals.

Willie: Distract El Supremo. Keep his mind off our friends. *(Suddenly)* I know exactly what to do. Ginny, you sneak up there and get those kids back to the entrance circle. I'll join you as soon as I've created a little—"diversion."

Ginny: OK. Be careful! *(She sneaks up left, hides behind a metal tree.* WILLIE *watches* SUPREME TECHNOCRAT *intently.* SUPREME TECHNOCRAT *places hands on* MIKE'*s helmet. There is a loud hiss.)*

SUPREME TECHNOCRAT: In a moment your minds will belong to me. *(Points to backdrop)* Into the treasury of my memory core will go all your knowledge, all your images and fantasies, all your rich past and present. And the future? Too bad. You have no future. Your minds will be as empty and blank as clean slates. But don't worry— I'll find some menial jobs for you – as Bits. *(He laughs wickedly.* WILLIE *leaps down center, waving his arms and yelling.)*

Willie: Hey there, people—it's party time! *(He sings loudly as he gyrates in place, snapping his fingers. All turn, observe* WILLIE, *astonished. As he dances,* COMMANDERS, BYTES, *and* BITS *form interested groups down left and right.* WILLIE *shows* BITS *how to clap.)* Clap, kids. *(*BITS *clap.)* Great! *(To a* BYTE*)* How about a dance? *(*WILLIE *whirls the* BYTE *around, then encourages other* BYTES *and* COMMANDERS.*)* Come on, guys. You can do it. Everybody get into the act—move those arms and legs. *(All dance clumsily.)* Beautiful! *(*TECHNOCRAT *strides down center, angrily.)*

SUPREME TECHNOCRAT: Commanders, I command you to cease this nonsense. *(All continue dancing, becoming looser, obviously enjoying themselves.)* That was a command, Commanders! *(They pay no attention.* TECHNOCRAT *raises hands. Hissing sound)* Cease! *(Thunderclap. All instantly drop to knees.* TECHNOCRAT, *arms folded, scowls at them.* WILLIE *signals to* GINNY. GINNY *runs to* MIKE, SHANNON, *and* PETER, *removes their helmets. They sway, as before, then recover themselves, rubbing eyes as if awakening.* GINNY *grabs* PETER*'s hand, urging them off.)*

Ginny: Let's go home, gang. *(She leads them off left.* WILLIE *retreats down center, on the apron, pursued by vengeful* TECHNOCRAT.*)*

SUPREME TECHNOCRAT: You demented creature! See what you have done? You have brought turmoil to my perfect world. I'll have your head for that. *(Reaches toward* WILLIE. *Hissing sound)*

Willie *(Putting arms on head protectively):* Don't you touch a hair on my head! You're nothing but a pirate, you know that? Only instead of doubloons and stuff, you hijack people's minds. But you made a big mistake, Technocrat. You left your amplifiers in our world. You just wait. Our scientists will swarm over here, and they'll smash your memory core to smithereens!

SUPREME TECHNOCRAT *(Gasping, staggering to throne, extending arms over backdrop, protectively):* Not my precious memory. The booty of a thousand raids throughout the cosmos is in this memory.

Shannon: We're home. Let's go. *(As she steps off the circle toward the basement scene,* WILLIE *pulls her back roughly.)*

Willie: No, Shannon! You could get lost in infinity. We can see home because we're in phase with our universe, but, look—there's no lighted entrance circle on the floor. My mother must have turned off the amplifier. We can't get back. *(He points to the amplifier. All groan.)*

Mike: You mean we're stuck here?

Peter: It looks that way. Even at the speed of light, we couldn't get home for centuries.

Ginny: There's nothing faster than light—except maybe thought.

Willie: Thought? Yes—thought! Maybe we can get through to my mother, with ESP. Remember that game of "Hot and Cold" we used to play when we were little?

Peter: Sure. I get it. We send "hot" and "cold" thoughts to your mom.

Willie: Right. Now, concentrate everybody. Our lives depend on it. *(To* MOTHER*)* Mom, it's Willie.

Mother *(Aside):* I wonder where that boy is? It's time for supper. *(She turns to exit.)*

Willie: Stay, Mom. Cold. Think cold, everybody. *(All concentrate fiercely on her.)*

All: You're cold—cold—cold.

Mother *(Shivering):* My goodness, it's freezing down here. Maybe I should turn on the furnace. *(She crosses to worktable.)*

Willie: Atta girl, Mom. Now, pick up the amplifier. Think hot, everybody. *(All concentrate again.)*

Mother *(Fanning herself):* Why, it's warm again. The heat seems to be coming from this. *(She picks up amplifier, curiously turning it in her hands.)*

Willie: Come on, Mom. Turn it on.

All *(Together):* Turn it on, turn it on, turn it on!

Mother: What is this thing? One of Willie's inventions, I suppose. *(She starts to put it on the table.)*

Willie *(Despairingly):* No, Mom—turn it on. *(To others)* Concentrate! *(All grimace in agonizing concentration.* MOTHER *renews her scrutiny of the amplifier.)*

Mother: I wonder how it works? I don't suppose it would hurt if I turned it on—just for a minute. *(She sets it on table.)*

Willie *(In anguish):* Please, Mom—

Mother: Here's the switch. *(Turns switch. Blackout. Thunderclap. Circle of light with everyone in it appears center. Lights go off on apron. Stage lights come up full.)* Willie Wurtzburger, you promised me you wouldn't blow the fuses. *(Short blackout. The amplifier is taken off. Spotlight out. Stage lights up full.)* There, you did it again!

Willie *(Rushing to embrace her):* Mom! Oh, Mom. I'm really sorry.

Mother *(Taken aback):* My goodness, Willie—it wasn't that serious. *(As others ad lib greetings)* Well, hi, kids. *(To* WILLIE*)* Why didn't you tell me the Science Club is meeting here tonight?

Willie: Must have slipped my mind, Mom. I've been a little busy.

Mother: Have a good time, everybody. Oh—there's lots of soda in the refrigerator. *(Exits)*

Mike *(Shaking* WILLIE*'s hand):* You've got a great mother, know that? *(*WILLIE *nods.)*

Ginny *(Pointing to worktable):* The amplifier's gone. Good riddance!

Shannon: We should do something, shouldn't we? Call a press conference, notify the newspapers. This is the story of the decade, maybe even the century.

Peter: You want to be the one to tell them the whole story, Shannon? They'll laugh you out of town.

Ginny: Wait a minute, guys. *(Bangs on worktable)* The meeting of the Science Club will come to order. *(All find boxes or cartons, form a semicircle around* GINNY.*)* First order of business—the letter from the Techno Company. *(She holds up letter, tears it to bits, triumphantly tossing the pieces into the air as all applaud.)*

Willie: Next order of business. I move we send out for pizza and have a party.

Mike: I second the motion. All in favor, say aye.

All: Aye. *(They applaud again.)*

Shannon: But what about the amplifier? That was a major breakthrough.

Willie: I don't think the world's ready for a million other universes. We've got all we can do to manage this one.

Shannon: But what if the Supreme Technocrat finds another way to get us?

Willie: Shannon, you worry too much. The Supreme Technocrat will have plenty of trouble with his own subjects. I should know. *(Crosses down center, dancing)* I taught them how to boogie! *(Dance music is heard.)*

All: All right! Go Willie! *(All start to dance. Quick curtain)*

Thinking About It

1. How many space creatures have you read about or seen on the screen? Are they all friendly? How do they compare with the ones in this play?

2. Every game has rules. Science fiction is like a game. What rules did the science fiction writer follow when she wrote *Journey to Technos?* Is one of the rules that everything must be scientifically accurate? What, then?

3. Become a playwright. Create Scene Five for *Journey to Technos.* You could describe what happens to the Supreme Technocrat, the Bits, Bytes, and Commanders. Or perhaps you'd prefer to have Willie or Ginny open a different box.

Another Science Fiction Book

In *The Wonderful Flight to the Mushroom Planet,* by Eleanor Cameron, an ad asks for two boys to build a very small spaceship. When David and Chuck answer the ad, they find a big adventure.

Set

It's May, 1980, and you're looking out the Time Machine's window at the peaceful mountain scene. That's about to change. Then prepare to be thrust back to the seaside town of Pompeii in A.D. 79. It won't be seen again for the next sixteen hundred years.

the Dial

THE DAY THE MOUNTAIN BLEW APART

by Chris Copeland

from *Challenge Plus Magazine*

It was like standing on a table with someone shaking it. I saw a puff of steam come out and then it looked like the whole mountain blew out sideways. The trees were shaking. It almost seemed like the sky was shaking. It was getting too black. The darkness was coming completely around us and over us. I was terrified that I wouldn't be able to breathe.

BEFORE

AFTER

Before and After

Jerry Wheeler was out for a weekend walk in Washington's Cascade Mountains when Mount St. Helens erupted on May 18, 1980. He was fifteen miles from the mountain. For Jerry, though, fifteen miles seemed too close.

Jerry managed to live through the eruption. Fifteen miles was just far enough away. David Johnston, a government scientist studying Mount St. Helens, was not so lucky. He was watching the volcano from a ridge top less than six miles away. David was just able to yell to his headquarters on the radio, "This is it! This is it!" After that, swept away by the blast, his radio went silent. David became one of the fifty-seven people killed by the volcano.

Less than a minute later, a whole world was blackened and lifeless. The gentle green valley that lay under the shimmering white peak of Mount St. Helens had disappeared. It was buried beneath smoking grey ash and thick black mud. Not even the colors survived.

Mounting Pressure

Mount St. Helens had been stretching and expanding for weeks before it exploded on May 18. Hot melted rock called *magma* had been rising inside the mountain. The pressure of the magma had pushed out the sides of the mountain three to five feet a day. Finally, like a balloon stretched to the breaking point, the mountain couldn't take any more pressure. It just blew.

Thousands of people rush out of buildings in Belgrade, Yugoslavia, as two strong earthquakes shake the area.

Unlike a balloon, the mountain exploded with the force of over forty million tons of dynamite. That's two thousand times the force of the atomic bomb that destroyed the Japanese city of Hiroshima in World War II. It was enough force to blow a quarter of a mile of earth off the top of the mountain, leaving a huge crater.

Along with the blast, a boiling hot mass of air rushed out of the volcano. The air was over 1,000° Fahrenheit—hot enough to melt glass. The heat instantly vaporized every living thing in its path. An instant later, a hurricane-force shock wave roared across the forested hills. It knocked down 200-foot-high trees as if they were toothpicks. Forests fifteen miles from the blast were flattened.

Covered in Ash

The source of Mount St. Helens's mighty belching lay deep inside the earth. There, the earth's *core,* or center, is so hot that it melts the rock around it. Streams of the melted rock, or magma, gradually rise up toward the earth's top layer, or *crust.* There, magma is under great pressure from the weight of the rock around it. This pressure causes not only volcanoes, but earthquakes too.

Right after Mount St. Helens erupted, tons of smoking ash and rocks tumbled out of the mountain's new crater. Melted snow and ice formed a huge mudflow. It pulled down trees, houses, and bridges. Floods of hot mud, rocks, and logs clogged many riverbeds and overflowed canyons.

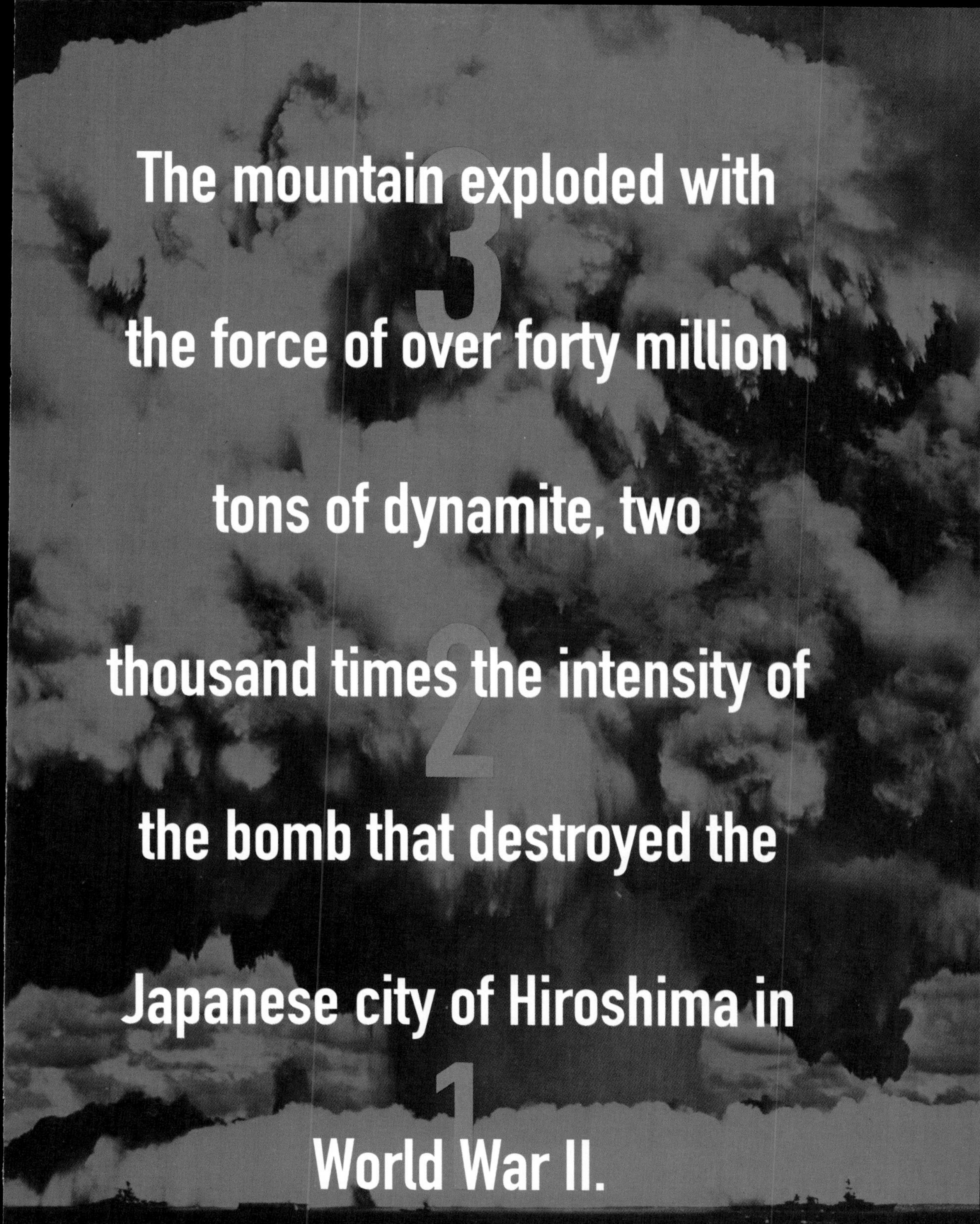

The mountain exploded with

the force of over forty million

tons of dynamite, two

thousand times the intensity of

the bomb that destroyed the

Japanese city of Hiroshima in

World War II.

Houses over twenty miles away from the crater were swept away by the black river. Toutle Lake Elementary School, thirty miles away, was buried in the mudflow. The students there had been practicing volcano drills for weeks. Luckily, Mount St. Helens picked a Sunday to blow up.

If the blast and mud were bad, the ash was worse. Mount St. Helens coughed out a cubic mile of the stuff. That's one ton for every person in the world.

Winds from the Pacific Ocean carried the ash over into eastern Washington. There it turned day into night. As far as five hundred miles from the volcano, the air was so thick with ash, you couldn't even see a person across the street.

The ash clogged everything—from car engines to people's throats. As Yakima (WA) resident Dale Davis discovered, "You had to dig it out of your mouth with your finger. You couldn't spit it."

School was cancelled for over a week in Yakima, eighty-five miles east of Mount St. Helens. But it wasn't really a holiday. Breathing the ash was so awful that no one went outside. Yakima turned into a ghost town overnight.

In the end, the ash from the volcano did the most damage. It completely buried the plants around Mount St. Helens. Almost nothing could grow in the stuff. The ash was like finely ground glass. It contained no nutrients, or food, for plants. Without plants to eat, many elk, deer, rabbits, and squirrels died.

Coming Back

Miraculously, strange little pockets of life survived the blast. A town of gophers (ground squirrels) was sheltered from the volcano's blast by a small ridge. Protected from the burning wind, these gophers survived, while their cousins for miles around died. The gophers then did their bit to bring back the forest. They dug up through the ash from their burrows underneath. Working like little plows, they pulled up rich soil to the surface where plants could use it.

Even the volcano's victims played a part in bringing the mountain back to life. Just a few months after the blast, scientists found elk bones poking up through the ash. All around the bones blossomed a thick patch of wildflowers. They were growing in the exact shape of the elk's body. These flowers couldn't grow anywhere else. But precious nutrients from the elk gave life to the new plants.

Today, ten years later, signs of life continue to poke through. Tough plants like thistles can manage to grow in the volcanic ash. Because of plants like these, the slopes of the mountain are starting to look green again. Frogs and salamanders from nearby streams are creeping back too.

But the trees are having a tougher time. The huge standing forest that was wiped out in the blast has barely sprouted again. Most trees need richer soil than weeds. So they must wait for other plants to improve the soil. Sometimes seedling trees *are* lucky enough to sprout in the ash, only to have hungry elk and deer chomp them down.

Foresters who have been watching Mount St. Helens since it erupted ten years ago say they have learned to be patient. One of them, Eugene Sloniker, puts it this way: "Nature takes its own time. It's going to be a long, slow process. There will eventually be a real forest again. But it may take more than a hundred years."

Another forester, John Fraenzi, has learned to see time in a new way. "Ten years is a long time to us," he says. "But it's nothing to Nature."

THINKING ABOUT IT

1

People are interested in natural catastophes. Why? Did reading about Mount St. Helens's catastrophe remind you of any others?

2

You are camping on Mount St. Helens several days before it explodes. What signs tell you that something is wrong?

3

If your time machine could take you to visit a natural catastrophe safely, would you choose to go? If so, which one would you visit? If not, which one would you avoid? Why?

Another Book About Mount St. Helens

The award-winning book *Volcano*, by Patricia Lauber, uses clear description and dramatic pictures to show what happened to Mount St. Helens and why.

PATRICIA LAUBER
VOLCANO
The Eruption and Healing of Mount St. Helens

At one house, slaves roasted a pig in the oven. A slave at another house fixed a lady's hair in the latest style.

A shopkeeper sold hot and cold drinks. A baker named Modestus put eighty-one loaves of bread in his oven. Gladiators relaxed in the wine shop. Priests ate their lunch of eggs and fish.

People gathered at Pompeii's Forum, or town center, and talked about the coming election. They read the news written on the walls the way people today read newspapers. Some bought fruit at the Forum market.

Then suddenly Vesuvius blew up, and the people ran from the Forum in every direction. The gladiators fled from the wine shop. The priests left their eggs and fish. The shopkeeper dropped money from the latest sale on the counter and hurried away. The baker darted off with flour still on his clothes. The lady forgot about having her hair styled and ran. The slaves left the pig roasting in the oven. The children stopped playing and screamed for their parents. And the dog twisted and pulled on his chain, but could not break loose.

About thirty minutes after the volcano erupted, a shower of hot ash poured down on the city. Pea-sized pieces of pumice, a lightweight rock filled with tiny holes, fell on everything and everyone.

A few people were hit by larger rocks torn from the volcano. Many tied pillows on their heads for protection against the hot ash and rocks. They shielded their faces with their hands or sleeves. The burning ash and rocks fell everywhere. The people of Pompeii seemed to be suffering through a nightmare—but they were wide awake.

Colosseum being built in Rome; when finished, it will be the largest amphitheater in the world.

Families stumbled along in darkness on the pumice-covered slabs of pavement toward the gates of the city. Parents and slaves carried small children. Many of Pompeii's twenty thousand people ran for their lives. They stampeded like animals. Some pushed their way through the sea gate hoping to escape by boat. Some freed horses or mules from carts and rode away on them.

Birds were killed in flight and dropped from the sky. Fish died at sea and washed on shore.

The wind blew ash and pumice all over the city—every hour six more inches piled up! By late afternoon a two-foot blanket of ash covered everything in Pompeii.

Roofs caved in from the weight of the ash and killed people under them. Bridges broke. Giant waves crashed against the shore. Ash fell into the harbor. It mixed with the water and turned to mush.

People who didn't leave right away had trouble opening their doors. Some chopped holes through the walls of their houses to escape.

Not everyone was able to leave Pompeii. Some people were too old or too sick. Others thought it would be safer to stay inside their houses. Some wasted precious minutes gathering up money and jewelry.

Those who waited too long never escaped.

Eyewitness Account

A navy admiral named Pliny the Elder watched the strange cloud from the Roman naval base at Cape Misenum, across the Bay of Naples from Vesuvius. Sometimes the cloud was white. Sometimes it was gray from the ash.

Pliny the Elder was an expert in science and had written a book called *Natural History*. He wanted to go closer to study the cloud and ordered a boat to take him across the bay. Before he left he heard that a friend was stranded at a beach town near Vesuvius. He ordered a warship to try to rescue as many people as possible.

His teenage nephew, Pliny the Younger, stayed behind in Misenum. After the eruption was over, Pliny the Younger heard about his uncle's rescue mission. He later wrote a letter to Tacitus, a historian who wanted to know what happened. This letter was published and can still be read today.

He wrote that Pliny the Elder "headed straight for the place of danger. He was entirely fearless. Ashes were already falling, hotter and thicker as the ship drew near."

The helmsman advised Pliny the Elder to turn back, but he kept going. Ash and floating pumice blocked the harbor where he planned to dock. He changed course and went ashore at the town of Stabiae, four miles south of Pompeii.

Fires blazed on the mountain. Pliny the Elder tried to make his friends feel less afraid. He told them the fires were only

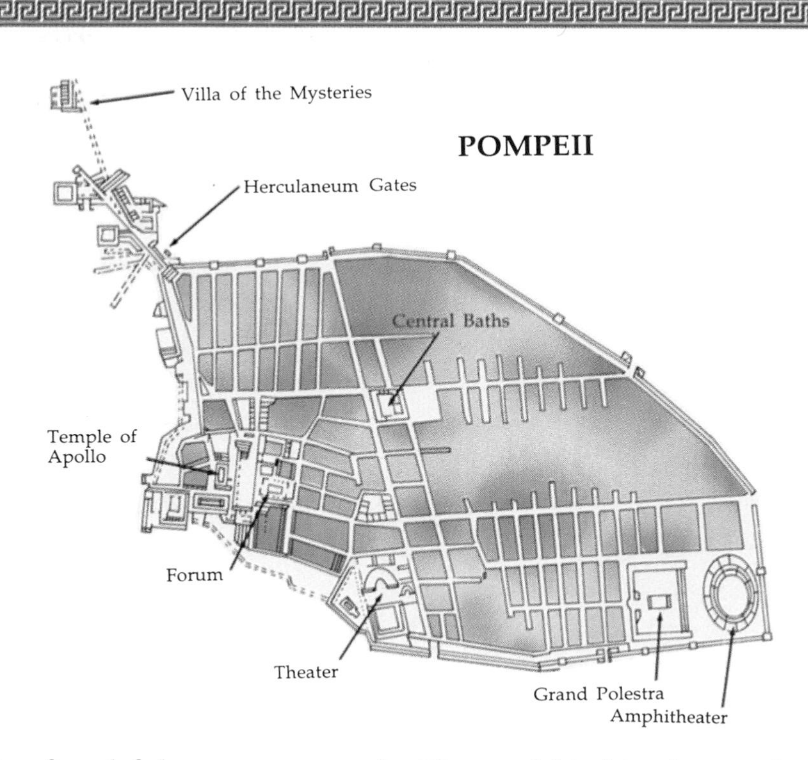

bonfires left by country people. Pliny and his friends went into a house. He lay down and took a nap to try to convince them there was nothing to worry about.

During the night, ash and pumice piled up outside the door of the room where Pliny slept. His friends woke him. They were afraid he might not be able to get out of the room if he stayed much longer.

The group argued about whether to stay inside or go out. Inside, the rooms trembled "with violent shocks." Outside, burning rocks fell.

They decided they would be safer outdoors. They tied pillows over their heads, took their lamps, and went out. Even though it was now morning, the ash made it so dark outside that it was "blacker . . . than any ordinary night."

Pliny the Elder wanted to take the people to safety in his warship, but the waves were too wild.

Ash from the volcano clogged his lungs, which were already weak. His friends spread a sheet on the ground for him to lie on. As he rested, he kept asking for cold water to drink.

Suddenly, there was a giant cloud of fire. People smelled sulfur and ran. Two slaves stayed behind and helped Pliny stand up. But he choked on the fumes and fell down dead. Some people who escaped from Stabiae told Pliny the Younger what happened.

Even in Misenum, Pliny the Younger felt the shocks from the volcano. He later described his own experiences in a second letter to the historian. "That night the shocks were so violent that everything felt as if it were not only shaken but overturned."

In the morning, the buildings rocked back and forth. Pliny the Younger and his mother left Misenum with many others from the town. Carts on the road slid in every direction. People put heavy stones in them to weigh them down, but the carts kept sliding.

In the cloud above Vesuvius, fire exploded like giant flashes of lightning. "The cloud sank and covered the sea. . . . Ashes were falling, and a thick black cloud came up behind spreading over the earth like a flood. . . . Then darkness fell . . . as if a lamp had been put out in a closed room."

Grown-ups and children screamed and shouted. "Some were calling to their parents, others to their children or to their wives, trying to recognize them by their voices. Some prayed for death. . . .

"Some thought the universe had fallen into darkness forever."

No Place to Hide

After Vesuvius erupted, the cloud of gas, ash, and stone shot into the air for about eighteen hours. Sometimes it rose as high as 12 miles (19 km). The ash fell on people as far away as Africa. Then the volcano's energy weakened for a while.

The long narrow cloud wobbled like the water from a hose when the pressure is turned down. About midnight a river of hot ash, rocks, and gas poured down the side of Vesuvius at 60 miles (96 km) an hour. This was called an avalanche. This avalanche did not come near Pompeii, but it buried Herculaneum, a city on the other side of Vesuvius.

Pressure from the volcano became stronger again, and the gases and ash shot into the air again. The cloud rose and fell. By six o'clock the next morning, three avalanches of hot ash, rocks, and gas had rushed down the mountain. Even though one hit the north wall of Pompeii, none went inside the walls. But ash and pumice had been falling on the city all night. Nine feet (2.7 m) of it was piled on top of everything.

Then, at 6:30 A.M. on August 25, another river of superheated gases, rocks, and ash crashed down the mountain. This time the avalanche went inside the walls of Pompeii. It tore off many roofs and knocked down everything higher than the 9 feet (2.7 m) of ash. The heat, ash, and gases clogged people's lungs and choked them to death. Gases even seeped inside the buildings.

Volcano expert Dr. Haraldur Sigurdsson has written that at about the same time this avalanche reached Pompeii, tons of very fine ash fell. The ash immediately buried everyone in the position they were when they died.

The fumes killed people inside their houses as well as outside. People held each other for comfort and were frozen with their arms around each other.

A woman died clutching her jewels. A slave died draped over plates he had dropped. A man begging outside the city gate died with his sack.

At least 2,000 people were killed and buried by the ashes covering Pompeii.

And the ash continued to fall.

Warning Signal

Seventeen years before Vesuvius exploded, a strong earthquake had rocked Pompeii.

The earthquake was a clue that Vesuvius was getting ready to erupt, but when it struck on February 5 in A.D. 62; people did not understand the warning. Vesuvius seemed to be a peaceful mountain; hardly anyone thought it was a volcano.

The earthquake was probably caused by pressure under the volcano. A volcano is a hole in the earth's crust that lets gases from inside the earth escape. Scientists think that about 40 miles (64 km) below the ground, heat melts the rock. When it does, gases are produced, and these gases in the melted rock try to escape. They push the hot melted rock, called *magma*, toward the surface of the earth.

As the magma moves up, it often forms a pipe to the surface. Pressure pushes the magma out through a hole in the ground. Once the melted rock gets outside the earth, it is called *lava*.

Sometimes the melted rock hardens in the pipe as it bubbles up. This hard rock blocks the opening and the gas cannot escape. The longer it has been since a volcano has erupted, the more blocked the hole is and the more pressure there is from trapped gas.

In the first century A.D. Vesuvius had not erupted for about 1,200 years. The pipe was so blocked, it needed a strong blast to clear it.

a five-century period of disunity.

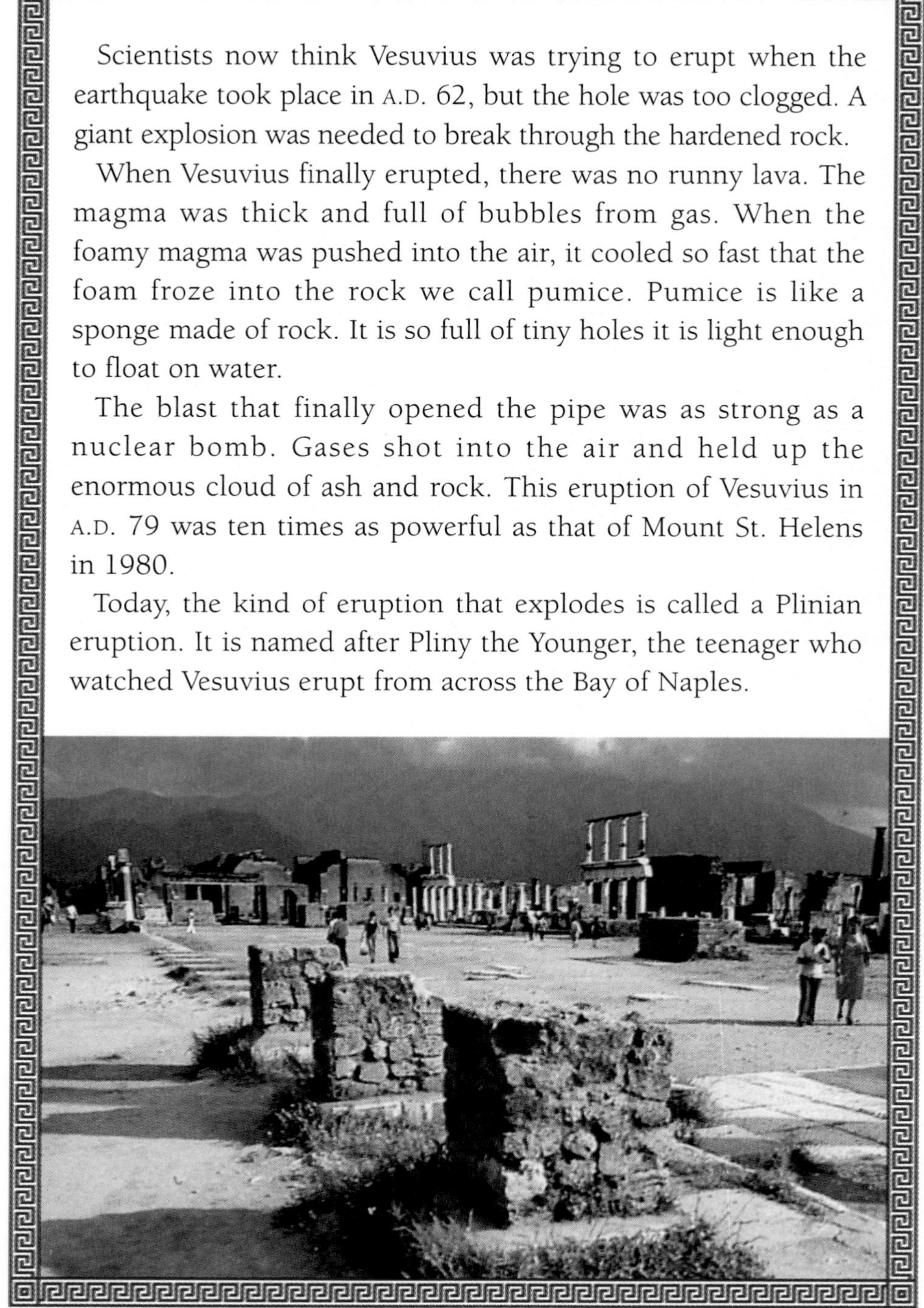

Scientists now think Vesuvius was trying to erupt when the earthquake took place in A.D. 62, but the hole was too clogged. A giant explosion was needed to break through the hardened rock.

When Vesuvius finally erupted, there was no runny lava. The magma was thick and full of bubbles from gas. When the foamy magma was pushed into the air, it cooled so fast that the foam froze into the rock we call pumice. Pumice is like a sponge made of rock. It is so full of tiny holes it is light enough to float on water.

The blast that finally opened the pipe was as strong as a nuclear bomb. Gases shot into the air and held up the enormous cloud of ash and rock. This eruption of Vesuvius in A.D. 79 was ten times as powerful as that of Mount St. Helens in 1980.

Today, the kind of eruption that explodes is called a Plinian eruption. It is named after Pliny the Younger, the teenager who watched Vesuvius erupt from across the Bay of Naples.

THINKING
ABOUT IT

1

THE PEOPLE BURIED BY VESUVIUS LIVED TWO THOUSAND YEARS AGO AND THOUSANDS OF MILES AWAY, YET IN MANY WAYS THEIR LIVES WERE LIKE OURS.

If you had been living in Pompeii in A.D. 79, what would you have been doing on August 24 at noon?

2

PLINY THE ELDER DIED BECAUSE OF HIS INTEREST IN SCIENCE—HE WANTED TO FIND OUT WHAT WAS HAPPENING.

He never knew, but now you know more than he did. Explain to Pliny the Elder how and why a volcano erupts.

3

QUICKLY TRAVEL TO POMPEII AND GIVE THE PEOPLE ONE ITEM FROM THE TWENTIETH CENTURY THAT YOU THINK WILL HELP THEM ESCAPE VESUVIUS.

Explain why your gift would save lives.

Gun Hill Rd
Gun Hill Rd
South Bronx

FRIENDS

FROM TAILS OF THE BRONX

by Jill Pinkwater

There is no place on earth like the Bronx. It's part of New York City, and I live there. My name is Loretta Bernstein. I live on Burnridge Avenue between the two 112s—112th Street and 112th Avenue.

I am ten years old. I am a short, skinny, Jewish, African American kid. My ancestors came from Ethiopia and were all black and Jewish too. We are called Falashas and are descended from the Queen of Sheba.

It's easy to tell who I am in a crowd because I wear big, round, red-framed eyeglasses all of the time and my official forest-ranger hat most of the time.

My claim to fame, besides having a famous ancestor, is that I am the only kid in the neighborhood who is going to be a forest ranger. I started working on my career when I was still practically a baby, studying the flora and fauna—that's plants and animals—at the New York Botanical Garden in the Bronx. I could identify most of the plants in the Perennial Garden long before I knew the names of most of my relatives. My friends say I will never become a ranger because it would mean that I would have to leave the Bronx. It *is* a problem, but I'll cross that bridge when I come to it. Meanwhile, a forest ranger is what I'm going to be.

Last year I earned two Master of Bugology certificates at the annual New York Botanical Garden Bug Hunt. I collected the most bugs *and* the greatest variety of bugs. It was no accident I won the contest. I've been on every one of the 250 acres of the Botanical Garden. I know where the bugs live, what they eat—and what eats them.

Everything important that has happened to me in my life has taken place in the Bronx—most of it on my block. That's because of the first Big Rule on Burnridge. If you're under eleven, you are not allowed off the block alone, except to go to school. *Alone* means without an adult. Being with a bunch of other kids doesn't count—no matter how many are with you.

The second Big Rule is: Be home before the streetlights go on. This is a tricky rule, because streetlights do not get turned on by a switch or even a timer. They're worked by

photoelectric cells. That means darkness and light turn them on and off. On cloudy days, especially in winter, the lights will sometimes kick on as early as four o'clock—catching everyone in the middle of important games or conversations. When that happens, there is a whole lot of yelling and screaming as kids race home. I've told my parents that it isn't fair for us kids to have our lives run by the weather. They tell me that nobody ever said life would be fair.

More than a hundred kids live on the block. I know them all, but mostly I hang out with my particular friends. Susan Quinn is my best friend. Her claim to fame is that she is the biggest nine-and-a-half-year-old in the entire neighborhood—and that includes both 112th Street *and* 112th Avenue, our school, and the Grand Concourse, which is nearby. She may be the biggest nine-and-a-half-year-old in the Bronx, but we haven't checked out the whole Bronx yet. The Bronx is a very large place. On the other hand, Susan Quinn is a very large kid—fat and tall. She'd get me if she heard me say *fat.* She prefers to describe herself as much bigger than usual.

Susan Quinn likes to be called Suzie Q. Suzie Q is a very tough kid. Nobody crosses her. When she was in third grade, a sixth-grade boy began calling Suzie Q "Gorilla" whenever he saw her. One day, when she had had enough, Suzie Q wrestled the kid to the ground and sat on his back for an entire lunch period. She made him say "Suzie Q" one thousand times. She made me do the counting. That was the last time anyone teased Suzie Q—to her face, at any rate.

The Raven is also a good friend of mine, even though he usually hangs around with older kids. He's Suzie Q's older brother. He's twelve, which means he's allowed off the block by himself. His claim to fame is that he is the only graffiti artist in the Bronx who works from a wheelchair. The Raven says his sitting position gives him an advantage because it puts him a couple of feet below where most of the other kids have used up blank wall space. The Raven does not draw on buses or subway cars or houses where people live. He says he is an urban artist who specializes in making the Bronx more beautiful, so mostly he decorates the walls of abandoned buildings. There are lots of those in our part of the Bronx.

The Raven is his graffiti name. It's also what he likes to be called. Sean is his real name, but he hasn't answered to it since he got his first spray can. The Raven is a major fan of Edgar Allan Poe, the famous Bronx poet. The Raven took his name from one of Poe's popular poems. Now that The Raven is allowed to travel around the Bronx alone, he visits Poe Park and Poe Cottage at least once a month.

The Raven's never been able to walk, but he gets around faster than any kid I've ever seen. He has racing wheels on his chair and always wears fingerless leather gloves so he can do wheelies or take off at top speed whenever he wants to. The Raven can go from a dead standstill to thirty miles an hour in less than ten seconds. He's faster than some cars in the neighborhood. The Raven's arms are very strong. He is the only kid on the block who can catch and hold on to Calvin when Calvin starts to run.

Calvin isn't exactly a friend. He's my brother. He's seven. It's my job to mind Calvin when we're outside. This isn't easy because Calvin's claim to fame is how fast he can run. He is the fastest runner at P.S. 46, our school. He can beat even the oldest kid on our block. When Calvin wants to leave the block, he leaves. Usually he just runs down 112th Street, along the Grand Concourse, up 112th Avenue, and back down Burnridge to our apartment house. On our block, that's a major crime for kids. So far Calvin has not had the nerve to cross any streets. Once he starts doing that, I think my parents are going to make me tie a rope around his waist and lead him around like a dog.

Anyway, if The Raven is around, Calvin can hardly make it to the corner even if he has a head start of half a block. This is important to me because if the Neighborhood Watch sees Calvin leave the block, a report is made to my parents. If Calvin leaves the block, I get the same punishment Calvin gets because I'm supposed to be minding him. To mind someone in the Bronx means to keep him in sight and out of trouble. No excuses. It's not fair, because Calvin is so fast and sneaky, but life in the Bronx can be tough.

That's what Julio Rodriguez says all the time. Julio's claim to fame is that he is the best-dressed, cleanest person on the block, in the neighborhood, in the Bronx, probably in New York City—all five boroughs—maybe in the United States. The Raven says it isn't normal for a kid Julio's age to be so unwrinkled and clean. Julio is ten, like me. If five of us go on an adventure in the alleys and basements of Burnridge Avenue, four of us will end up covered with dirt and grime and soot. Sometimes one of us will rip a shirt or a jacket on something sharp. Not Julio. Never Julio.

Julio wears a silver chain around his neck. On it is his good-luck charm—a small, silver rabbit's foot. His grandmother gave it to him. He says it protects him from bad guys and dirt. We make fun of Julio and his magic charm.

Julio doesn't care. He says as long as he stays clean and pressed and free of bruises, we can laugh all we want. Julio insists that since he started wearing the charm, not one bad kid in the Bronx has bothered him.

I like Julio. He and I plan adventures together. He calls us co-conspirators and says we share a psychic wavelength. That means we think alike. Julio is the smartest kid I know. He studies the dictionary and learns three new words every night. Sometimes, when Julio uses two or three of his dictionary words in a sentence, the rest of us have no idea what he is talking about. Julio also speaks Spanish—mostly to his grandmother. He says that considering the neighborhood we live in, there is no excuse for all of us not to know at least one language besides English. He even thinks Suzie Q should learn Gaelic.

The first time he told her that, Julio had to explain to Suzie Q that Gaelic is the ancient language of Ireland, the place Suzie Q's ancestors came from. Suzie Q was sitting on Julio's stomach as he spoke because she thought he had said "eat garlic," not "speak Gaelic." Suzie Q took it as an insult and threw Julio to the ground as punishment.

"Your rabbit's foot didn't protect you from Suzie Q," I said after Julio had brushed himself off.

"Suzie Q is not a bad guy," he said. "She is simply a monolingual lout of my acquaintance." Then a clean, unwrinkled Julio smiled at Suzie Q and sauntered off. An embarrassed Suzie Q ignored his remark.

That night I looked up *monolingual* and *lout* in the dictionary. I kept my findings to myself. I like Julio.

population of about 200,000, mostly descendants of Irish and German immigrants.

Anthony DeRosa is my next-door neighbor and the best-looking boy in the Bronx. He is an only child. We are the same age and have always lived in the same building. Anthony and I are like brother and sister. We're also very good friends. This means we argue a whole lot but never stay mad for long.

Anthony's claim to fame is that he knows more about the people on the block than they know about themselves. He spends huge amounts of his time collecting the life stories of everyone he meets. Anthony is the favorite kid of all the older people on Burnridge. He's really interested in listening to them—especially if they are talking about their troubles. They tell him *everything*—about themselves and about others. In their eyes, Anthony DeRosa can do no wrong—and believe me, he does plenty.

Kids tell Anthony things too—secret stuff they never thought they'd say out loud. When Anthony listens to someone, he really *listens.* I don't know how he does it, but as soon as he fixes those big brown eyes on someone, that person begins talking. He's our main source of block information—like a daily news broadcast. I figure that someday Anthony will be a famous psychiatrist or detective or FBI agent or spy or reporter. He certainly has the right talent.

Finally, there is Rochelle Firestone. I can't exactly call her a friend; she's just with us most of the time—uninvited. Rochelle's claim to fame is that she is the richest kid and the worst snob on the block. She says her family is homesteading on Burnridge, like pioneers. I remember the first time Rochelle announced that her family was "turning the tide" and opening our block to what she called other upwardly mobile families. We turned our backs on her and walked away.

"Does she think the rest of us are downwardly mobile?" Julio asked, looking angry.

"What does that mean?" asked Calvin.

"That we're losers," Julio answered.

"My dad says that even though the families on Burnridge are hardworking, most of us are just a few paychecks away from being homeless," said Suzie Q.

"He said 'used to be,' " The Raven corrected his large baby sister. "Now that we have the Neighborhood Association, we're not so . . . so . . . "

"Vulnerable," Julio helped.

"Still, it's scary," I said. "What if my dad lost his job?"

"Mommy works too," said Calvin.

"My mom isn't working now because of the baby." Suzie Q sounded very worried.

Rochelle showed up, so we changed the topic. None of us wanted to give her the satisfaction of knowing we were upset by anything she did or said. But we've talked about our worries many times since. It helps to have friends you can share things with—even awful things.

Anyway, back to Rochelle. None of my friends really likes her much, but since her first day on the block, she's hung on to Suzie Q like a leech. Rochelle bribes Suzie Q with junk food. In exchange, Suzie Q doesn't let the rest of us destroy Rochelle when she says something snotty or nasty. Remarks come out of Rochelle's mouth at the rate of about four or five an hour. Some days Suzie Q has to really work to earn her candy bars and pizza slices. If it weren't for Suzie Q, Rochelle would have been history a week after her family moved here.

My friends and I do a lot of hanging around the block together. Not a single one of us has a personal television, or computer, or stereo system. As you have probably figured out, there isn't a whole lot of extra money on Burnridge Avenue. Two of us have bicycles, and we all have our own radios—small ones, not Bronx Blaster Boxes. Except Rochelle, of course. She has a room full of every toy that has ever been advertised on television. I saw her room once when she first moved in. It was like visiting a store. We played for about an hour with Rochelle's stuff—until I got bored and restless. It was a new experience for me. I had never been bored in my life. I began questioning Rochelle.

I discovered what Rochelle didn't have was anything practical—like the things needed for playing in the street. She didn't have a pink Spalding ball, or a clothesline rope, or white chalk, or a wax-filled bottle cap, or jacks, or marbles, or skates with metal wheels. Rochelle didn't even own a yoyo. It was pitiful. Unfortunately, her mother did have an empty can, and that's why I got banned from Rochelle's house forever.

I wasn't thinking bad thoughts about Rochelle when we went outside that day. I hardly knew her. I was just being polite when I asked for the can. I was trying to teach Rochelle about the kind of sports equipment we use on Burnridge. I was about to toss the can into the trash when Anthony spotted it in my hand. He began yelling, "Kick the can, kick the can!" Kids appeared from nowhere. Bottle caps were pocketed as skelly games were stopped. Marbles were scooped off manhole covers. A double-dutch contest, a stoopball game, a hopscotch match, and at least three games of jacks ended in an instant. Spaldings and yoyos were stashed as at least fifty Burnridge kids massed at the Firestone stoop.

"Come on, guys," Suzie Q pleaded, "she doesn't know anything. She's just a ignorant yuppie kid."

"*An* ignorant yuppie kid," corrected Julio.

"So what," everyone else shouted. "She's new on the block, and she's *it.*"

"You're right. It's the law of the Bronx," said Suzie Q, backing away from Rochelle.

"Life in the Bronx can be tough," said Julio, picking an invisible piece of dust off his shirt.

The kids spread out on the street.

"You're it," I said to Rochelle. I felt responsible and was feeling a little guilty.

"Is it hide-and-seek?" she asked nervously. She had already told me that she was afraid of basements and most other dark places.

"It's kick the can." I explained the game to her: She had to guard the can using only her feet, keeping it from being stolen by the other kids, *and* tag one other kid while the can was in her possession.

"Simple," said Rochelle. "When someone tries to steal the can, I'll tag them. No big deal."

"Hah!" I answered. "If someone else kicks the can while you're tagging another kid, you're still it. You can take the can along with you by kicking it—like in soccer. But you can't pick it up."

"Easy. Fun," said Rochelle.

"Look, Rochelle, if a kid steals the can from you while you're it, you have to steal it back before you can tag someone." My guilt was fading fast.

"This game is for simpletons." Rochelle put the can on the ground. Guilt totally gone, I took off.

Kick the can is what is done to new kids on Burnridge. There is no way on earth a kid can win against all the kids on a block. Everyone who is outside usually plays—even kids as young as five can join in. If the person leaves the can to tag someone, another kid rushes in and kicks it. Then the other kids bat the can back and forth—keeping it from the person who is *it.* Kick the can, like ring-a-levio, can go on all day.

The difference is that ring-a-levio, a complicated kind of hide-and-seek, is played with two teams, the larger the better. Kick the can is a neighborhood initiation—one kid against everyone else. Usually we end the game by carrying the new kid—who has collapsed onto the pavement—to the corner, pooling our change and treating him or her to as much pizza or ice cream as our money will buy. To be accepted on our block, all a kid has to do is show heart and good humor.

After about fifteen minutes of being *it*, a very sweaty Rochelle finally realized what the game was all about. Instead of sticking with it, she picked up the dented can and, in an awful snit, stomped into her house.

"She took the can," said one kid.

"That's creepy," said another.

"A real toad," said a third.

"Who gets the pizza?" asked Suzie Q.

"She'll never last," Anthony predicted.

Rochelle's mother slammed out of her front door and hollered to me, "Loretta Bernstein, you are an ill-mannered ingrate. You may never again enter this house. You and your ruffian friends are banned. Forever." She closed the door.

"Did she call us a name?" asked Suzie Q.

"She called Loretta two names, I think," said Calvin.

"I counted a total of three," said Julio.

"What did I do?" I asked.

"You provided the can," said Julio.

"Actually, Rochelle's mother gave it to me," I said.

"Nice going," said Anthony. The streetlights came on and we all raced home.

You have to admit that we are an interesting bunch of kids—even if some of us are obnoxious. That's a word I learned from Julio.

THINKING ABOUT IT

1.

If you lived on Burnridge Avenue in the Bronx, how would you fit in? What would your claim to fame be?

2.

Explain to Rochelle's mother what is going on. Explain about the kick-the-can game. Explain the way the neighborhood kids are acting toward Rochelle.

3.

Imagine you can choose when and where you live. Would you live on Burnridge Avenue in the Bronx *now?* Would you choose another place and time? Explain.

ANOTHER BOOK ABOUT KIDS IN A CITY

In *City Kids in China,* by Peggy Thomson, you can find out how Ming, Liu, and other children live in the modern city of Changsha.

DIXIE
QUEEN
PLUG
CUT
SMOKING
TOBACCO

TIME: 1840-1890

PIONEER CHILDREN IN THE WEST

by Russell Freedman

At a frontier school in California, a boy was having trouble with his studies. His notebooks were a mess. His face was always smeared with ink. When he was called on to recite, his memory failed him. Years later his teacher, Prentice Mulford, recalled the student.

"He would hold a pen as he would a pitchfork. . . . He was not a regular scholar. He was sent to school only when it was an 'off-day' on his father's ranch. In the scholastic sense, he learned nothing.

"But that boy at the age of fifteen would drive his father's two-horse wagon, loaded with fruit and vegetables, 150 miles from California to Nevada over the rough mountain roads of the Sierras, sell the produce to the silver miners of Aurora and adjacent camps, and return safely

◀Pioneer schoolgirls at lunch

home. He was obliged in places to camp out at night, cook for himself, look out for his stock, repair harness or wagon and keep an eye out for skulking Indians."

Scholars or not, frontier youngsters learned to take on responsibilities early in life. They began to help out around the homestead as soon as they were old enough to follow instructions. A pioneer family needed all the help it could get.

Small children were expected to feed the chickens, gather the eggs, weed the vegetable garden, and pick wild nuts, berries, and fruits. As they grew older, they joined in the heavier work of plowing and planting, tending livestock, hauling water, pitching hay, building cabins and fences, hunting and trapping, cooking, washing, and cleaning.

As a rule, girls helped their mothers with the endless household tasks, while boys labored in the fields with their fathers. When necessary, girls and their mothers did heavy farm work. Boys and their fathers washed clothes and learned their way around the kitchen.

Margaret Mitchell was an able-bodied girl on a Kansas homestead during the 1870s: "There were nine children in our family, six girls and three boys, and as the girls were older and my father not strong, the hard toil of the pioneer life fell to the lot of the girls. We used to set traps on the banks city of 25,000 people, many of whom have come to seek gold during the California gold rush.

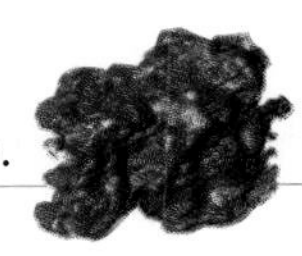

of the Republican and caught wolves, badgers, bobcats and skunks. Wild turkeys were very plentiful then, and we sometimes used traps to catch them.

"We had some very interesting and thrilling experiences with some of the animals we caught. One day an older sister and I were out looking at our traps and noticed that a big bobcat that was caught had climbed a tree with the chain hanging to him. I sat and watched him while my sister went for a gun and shot him. . . .

"Our house was made of logs, and the girls all helped with the construction of it. The cave we made ourselves and were justly proud of the work, for no one in our neighborhood had a better one."

An important chore on every homestead was hauling the family's daily water supply. Water had to be brought from a well, a spring, or the nearest creek, which might be a mile away. Big wooden buckets filled with water were hung at either end of a yoke. Balancing the yoke on his shoulders, a boy (or girl) would trudge back to the cabin with the buckets swinging and the water sloshing.

Another regular job was keeping the stove and fireplace supplied with fuel. Where there was enough timber, youngsters gathered and chopped firewood. On the treeless plains, they collected anything that might burn—twigs, grass and hay, sunflower stalks, dried corncobs. The most common fuel on the plains was buffalo or cow chips—chunks of dried manure left by the grazing herds. Children were sent out to gather this precious fuel in big baskets and wheelbarrows. The chips were carried home, stored in old gunnysacks, and tossed into the cookstove as needed.

Children helped care for the barnyard animals. They fed and watered the livestock, milked the cows and goats, herded the hogs and sheep. Sometimes they made games out of their chores. One girl was put in charge of the family's hogs, with her little brother as a helper. They gave each hog a name. "I used to make my brother believe that they were talking when they grunted," she recalled. "I was able to understand their hog Latin and I would interpret to him."

Just about every Western child learned to handle a horse. Youngsters on horseback drove cows to pasture and went galloping off on errands. Often a boy or girl would manage a two- to four-horse team pulling a wagon or plow. On cattle ranches, youngsters were sent on long rides to mend fences, inspect water holes, and search for lost calves. A British visitor to the frontier advised his countrymen back in England: "Learn to ride as soon as you possibly can. A man or boy who cannot ride is, in a new country, about as valuable as a clerk who cannot write in a city office."

Ordinary household chores took up a great deal of time on a pioneer homestead. Long hours were spent in the kitchen canning fruit, preserving meat, baking bread, roasting coffee beans, churning butter. Families made their own candles, their own soap, and their own home remedies. Children drank buttercup tea for asthma. They swallowed cough syrup made from onions mashed in sugar. When they had a fever, they were rubbed down with a salve of skunk grease mixed with turpentine.

Much of the pioneers' clothing also was made at home. On quiet evenings, girls sat by the fireside with their mothers, sewing skirts and trousers, knitting sweaters and socks, fashioning leather hats, coats, and shoes. They stitched window curtains, stuffed pillows, and embroidered linens. And they worked on handmade quilts that are so beautiful, some of them can be seen today in many museums.

Thinking About It

1. If you were a parent in the pioneer West, would you make your children work so hard? Why or why not? What would your choices be?

2. For pioneer children in the West, work and play were not always opposites. Based on what you've just read, what tasks may have seemed like play as well as work? How could you show that they could be play as well as work?

3. You are a frontier child living 125 years ago. You are to design a quilt that will show people in A.D. 2000 what you and your brothers and sisters did in your childhoods. You can't show everything, so select the most important and interesting jobs and events for the "Quilt of Our Lives."

More on the West by Russell Freedman

In Children of the Wild West, Russell Freedman tells about the daily lives—work, play, and school—of children from many different backgrounds who lived there.

Why do people get so excited about playing games?

Final Stops:

The modern Olympics and a ball field in Mexico in A.D. 200.

To reserve your seat for a future voyage...

open any

book!

THE MODERN OLYMPICS

BY NATE AASENG

For more than a thousand years, the ancient town of Olympia in western Greece was the gathering place for the greatest athletes of the world. Every four years, nations stopped their wars while men boxed, ran, jumped, and threw objects in the first Olympic stadium.

First prize was a wreath of olive—and fame throughout the land. After the ancient Olympic Games were banned by the Roman emperor in the year 394, the Olympian ideal of peaceful athletic competition among the nations became a distant memory. The stadium and temples of Olympia fell into ruin.

Baron Pierre de Coubertin

About 1,500 years later, in the nineteenth century, a group of German archaeologists began to dig in the area of Olympia. Many people around the world read about the ancient buildings that were being dug up. Scholars and students studied historical writings and learned how the ancient Games had been organized. They even discovered the names of some of the great athletes who had competed in the Games. Finally, in 1896, a group of sports fans set out to bring the Games back to life.

Most of the pieces for this noble experiment had already been assembled. The Games had a tireless organizer (Baron Pierre de Coubertin), a host country (Greece), financing

The Greek marathon runner approaches the finish line in the 1896 Olympics.

(courtesy of a wealthy Greek architect), and competitors (more than 300, from thirteen different nations).

At first, the Games failed to inspire. The athletic performances of the 1896 Athens Olympics seemed very ordinary compared to the stories of legendary heroes who had battled for Olympic honors in ancient Greece. As the Games progressed, the failure of the host country to win any track and field events added to the disappointment of the fans. After lying dormant for 1,500 years, the Olympic Games needed something extraordinary to bring them back to life.

Late in the competition, on April 10, 1896, a small

discovers radioactivity. | Tootsie Rolls, the first penny candy to be wrapped in paper, are introduced in New Yo

group of men gathered at the Marathon Bridge. Marathon, a village north of Athens, was the site of an ancient Greek victory over Persian invaders in 490 B.C. According to a story passed down through the years, a Greek messenger had run all the way from the battlefield to Athens with news of the victory. After giving his report, the runner had collapsed and died from exhaustion. In honor of this legend, Baron de Coubertin had introduced a new event called the marathon. The runners would follow the road from Marathon to Athens, an incredible 40 kilometers (about 25miles) away.

Nearly 100,000 spectators gathered at the stadium to witness the finish. All afternoon they anxiously awaited reports of the race's progress. Unfortunately, the early news was no more promising for Greece than the results of any of the other events had been. A French athlete named Lermusiaux had dominated the early portion of the race. Unable to maintain his own pace, Lermusiaux slowed, gave up the lead to Edwin Flack of Australia, and soon collapsed. A subdued Greek crowd passed along the latest information—Flack was just a few miles away and holding on to his lead.

Four kilometers from the finish line, Flack, a gold medalist in the 800 meters, faltered. Soon after, a Greek army major charged into the stadium on horseback to deliver the latest bulletin to the king and queen of Greece: A Greek was in the lead!

The news spread rapidly throughout the stadium. Sports fans, who had been mildly curious onlookers, became excited and tried to the Mexicans' hopes were evaporating. Muñoz, swimming in fourth place, appeared out of contention. Suddenly, the young swimmer surged forward. As he moved into third place, the hometown fans began cheering loudly. The inspired Muñoz continued to catch up to Kosinsky.

All spectators were on their feet as Muñoz touched the wall for the final turn just inches behind Kosinsky. Amid indescribable bedlam, the teenager caught the Soviet halfway down the final length and touched home half a second ahead of him to claim the gold medal.

In the celebration that followed, Muñoz was pulled out of the water and carried around the pool area. Spectators hugged and kissed each other. Television announcers wept openly. The Olympics had again provided hometown sports fans with an unforgettable experience.

Every four years, thousands of the world's greatest athletes gather to compete in the Olympic Games. The grandeur and the massive scale of the Summer Olympics have made it the world's greatest showcase for what the human body and willpower can accomplish.

THINKING ABOUT IT

1.

You are suddenly at the Olympic Games of the year 2004. Are you an athlete? What event are you in? Are you a spectator? What event are you watching? Why did you choose what you did?

2.

The Olympic Games are going to be held in your city, and you have been put in charge of getting everything ready. What has to be done?

3.

How might a radio announcer describe one of the races told about in this selection (in the 1896 Olympics or the 1968 Olympics) as it is happening? Be an announcer and call the "play-by-play."

BOOKS ABOUT THE OLYMPICS

Both *Great Summer Olympic Moments* and *Great Winter Olympic Moments,* by Nate Aaseng, describe some of the most dramatic people and finishes of the Olympics.

MAYA BALLPLAYERS

FROM *FACES MAGAZINE*

BY PETER KVIETOK

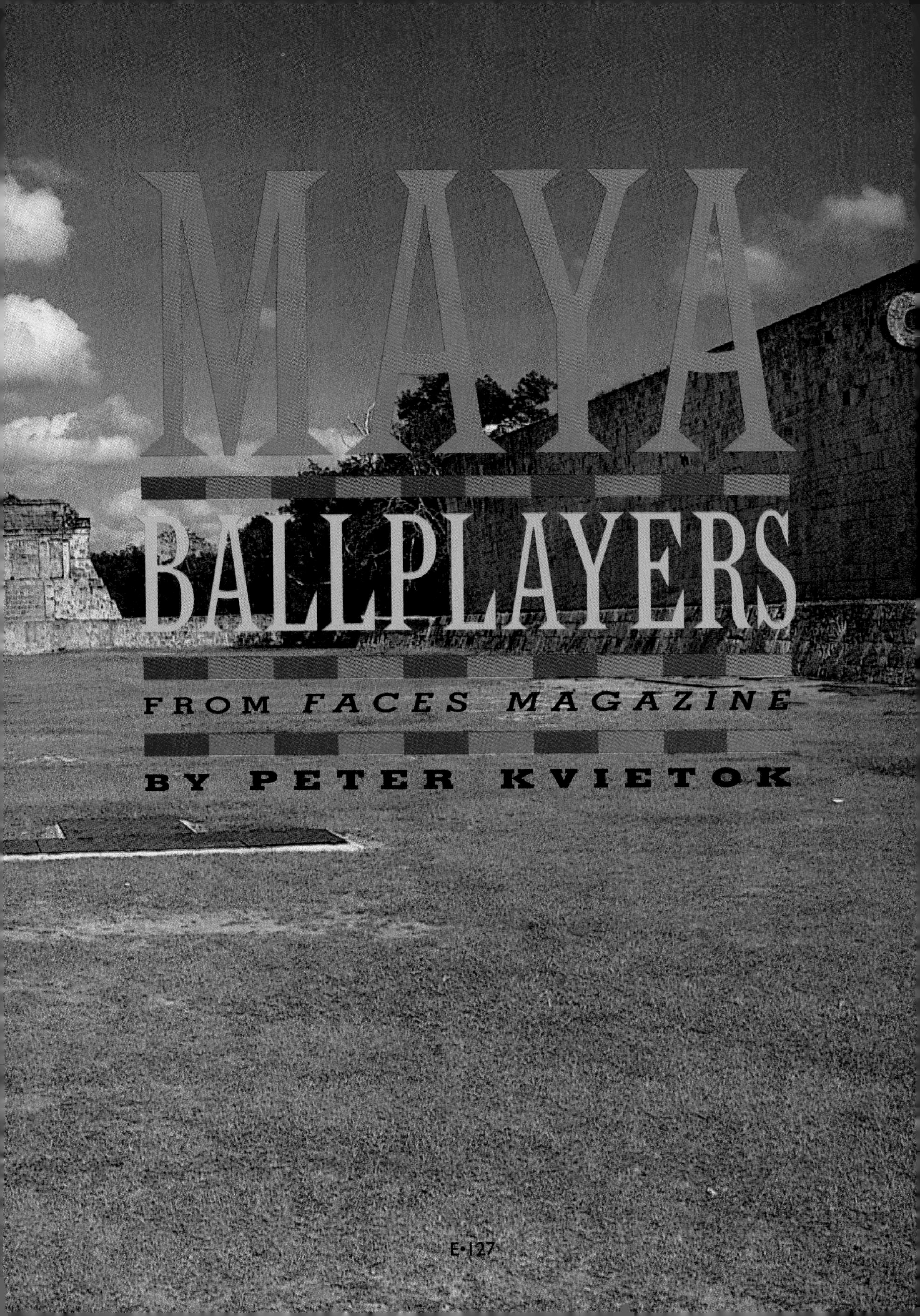

"The boys took their ball and went to the court where their father had played. They happily played the sacred game and the earth shook beneath their running feet. Below the earth, the Lords of Death looked around. Who dares disturb us by playing ball above our heads? The Lords called their messengers. Go tell those who play ball up there that the Lords of Death wish to see them. Tell them to come within seven days and to bring their ball and gear so that we may play together."

This is part of a story told in the *Popol Vuh,* an ancient Maya book of religious myths. In the story, two boys go to the underworld to play a ball game against the Lords of Death. The boys win their matches, but the gods play many dangerous tricks on them. The boys are very smart, however, and avoid the danger until one of them has his

Figure of a Chac-Mool, Chichén Itzá, Yucatán

The courts differed according to where the game was played. A site in Mexico called Chichén Itzá had a very large court with a temple at each end. The playing field was in the shape of the letter I and was 500 feet long, 120 feet wide at its narrowest part, and 207 feet wide at the ends, about the size of ten standard tennis courts. In Guatemala, the courts were smaller but very well made with stone and plaster. Courts in the West Indies had low stone walls and were not very fancy. European reports mention simple courts in Mexico and the West Indies, but we do not know much about how they looked because only the fancy ones have survived.

The name of the game, pok-ta-pok, refers to the ball, which was made of natural rubber from the sap of a tree. Probably the world's first rubber ball, it could bounce very high, like the "superballs" you can buy

Maya ballplayer

today, and could be as large as a volleyball. Because it was so big and dense, the players had to wear protective equipment to keep from being hurt and to be able to hit the ball harder. Athletic equipment included belts, chestpads, armpads, kneepads, heavy deerskin trousers and tunics, sandals, back shields, and hand and wrist protectors. Without this protection, a fast ball could probably kill someone. To return a low ball, the players had to throw themselves on the hard plaster floor, so the thick trousers and kneepads were very important for safety. In addition to this equipment, some players would wear fancy head-dresses, necklaces, nose ornaments, and ear plugs during ceremonial games.

The game probably had very complicated rules, but it is impossible to tell exactly how people played it a thousand years ago. We do know that players would hit the ball using their hips, buttocks, thighs, elbows, wrists, and chests. Hands and feet were not allowed to touch the ball. Imagine playing any ball game without using your hands or feet! Several versions of the game were played, but most involved hitting the ball back and forth between two sides of a court, like volleying in tennis or volleyball. A team would lose points if the players were unable to return the ball correctly. You might lose points if you hit the ball out of bounds or if you let the ball hit the ground on your side of the court.

Some surviving courts have small stone rings attached to the tops of the side walls. These may have been used for scoring, although it would have been very difficult to hit a

BOOKS TO ENJOY

A BRUSH WITH MAGIC
by William J. Brooke Harper Collins, 1993
There is magic in the simplest things, in a sunset over the blue ocean, in the singing of a song. For Liang, a boy in ancient China, magic is the paintbrush found with him as a baby in a basket down by the rice paddies.

MATT GARGAN'S BOY
by Alfred Slote Lippincott, 1975
Danny Gargan has big plans for his baseball team and for getting his parents back together. Now it looks as if Susie Warren and her dad will ruin everything.

POMPEII
by Ron and Nancy Goor Crowell, 1986
Photographs and drawings depict the horror of the eruption of Mt. Vesuvius as well as give a glimpse of everyday life in a Roman town.

BULL RUN
by Paul Fleischman Harper Collins, 1993
Journey back to the Battle of Bull Run. This account of the first battle of the Civil War weaves hopes, horrors, and folly and lights the faces behind dates and facts.

THE BIG WAVE

by Pearl Buck Harper Collins, 1973

When the volcano erupts, the big wave will surely follow. Will the villagers obey the warning bell and leave their homes for the safety of the Old Gentleman's hilltop castle?

THE RIDDLE OF THE ROSETTA STONE

by James Cross Giblin Crowell, 1990

Uncovering the secret of the Rosetta Stone was quite a challenge. Read the story of scholars' painstaking progress toward understanding the mysteries of ancient Egypt.

JERUSALEM, SHINING STILL

by Karla Kuskin Harper Collins, 1987

The story of the city of Jerusalem is an exciting one. For over four thousand years, people have fought over the city and tried to claim it as their own. Through it all this special city has survived.

CIRCLE OF GIVING

by Ellen Howard Atheneum, 1984

When Marguerite's family moves to Los Angeles, she is miserable! Through her friendship with Francie, a girl with cerebral palsy, Marguerite sees how things can change.

LITERARY TERMS

FIGURATIVE LANGUAGE Figurative language is any use of language that goes beyond the literal, everyday meaning of words. "How I Faced the Hampshire Mauler" includes many examples of figurative language: simile ("Max goes for books like a hungry piranha goes for toes"), metaphor ("this is Opportunity Knocking"), idiom ("I broke the ice by writing her"), and exaggeration ("the best-looking girl west of the Mississippi").

IMAGERY An author uses imagery to let readers know how things look, sound, smell, taste, or feel. The author of "Pompeii: Nightmare at Midday" describes the volcanic blast as spreading out "like an umbrella" and the violent shocks feeling as though everything had been overturned. These images give you a vivid idea of what the volcanic eruption was like.

PARODY A parody is an imitation of a story or common idea, changing it enough so it becomes ridiculous and, usually, funny. *Journey to Technos* is a parody of space-travel stories. There are stereotyped characters such as a tyrannical ruler, zombie-like guards, and cruel commanders. The tone of this parody is humorous; its purpose is to entertain.

SCIENCE FICTION In a science fiction story, scientific laws and technological inventions play an important part. The events that happen generally are fantastic—they could not possibly occur. "How I Faced the Hampshire Mauler" is a good example of science fiction because the story's action depends on the use of one fantastic invention—a time machine. *Journey to Technos* is similar; the characters use technology, and the idea of an alternate universe is so fantastic.

THEME The theme is the idea that runs throughout a story and holds it together. Sometimes this basic, main idea is stated by the author, and sometimes it is not. There is usually more than one way to state a story's theme. The theme of "Friends" could be "People of different backgrounds and personalities make a neighborhood interesting." How else could you state the theme?

TIME-TRAVEL FANTASY A fantasy is a story that could not happen. In time-travel fantasy, characters must cross into different time periods—an act that just is not possible. Authors usually have their characters get to other time periods by using devices such as time machines or common objects such as doors or mirrors.

G L O S S A R Y

Vocabulary from your selections

ban (ban), **1** forbid by law or authority; prohibit: *Swimming is banned in this lake.* **2** the forbidding of an act or speech by authority: *The city has a ban on parking cars in this busy street.* 1 *v.*, **banned, ban ning;** 2 *n.*

chain mail (chān māl), kind of flexible armor, made of metal rings linked together. *n.* Also, **chain-mail.**

cham pi on (cham′pē ən), **1** person, animal, or thing that wins first place in a game or contest: *He is the swimming champion of our school.* **2** person who fights or speaks for another; person who defends a cause: *That writer is a great champion of peace. n.*

com pli ance (kəm plī′əns), **1** a giving in or agreeing; yielding to a request or command: *I appreciated the clerk's ready compliance with my request to exchange the sweater.* **2** tendency to yield to others: *His refusal was all the more surprising in view of his usual compliance. n.*

crater (def. 2)

cra ter (krā′tər), **1** a bowl-shaped hole around the opening of a volcano. **2** hole on the surface of the earth, moon, etc., shaped like this: *The meteor crashed to earth, forming a huge crater. n.*

dense (dens), **1** closely packed together; thick: *a dense forest, a dense fog,* **2** having a quantity of matter in a unit of volume or of area: *Iron is a very dense material. Styrofoam is not dense. adj.,* **dens er, dens est.** **—dense′ly,** *adv.* **—dense′ness, den′si ty.** *n.*

dom i nate (dom′ə nāt), control or rule by strength or power: *She spoke with the authority needed to dominate the meeting. v.,* **dom i nat ed, dom i nat ing.**

dor mant (dôr′mənt), **1** sleeping; seeming to sleep; not moving or feeling: *Animals that hibernate are dormant during the winter.* **2** without activity; not in motion, action, or operation: *Many volcanoes are dormant. adj.*

e rup tion (i rup′shən), a bursting or throwing forth: *There was an eruption of glowing melted rock from the mountaintop. n.*

fal ter (fôl′tər), not go straight on; draw back or hesitate; waver: *I faltered for a moment before I made my decision. v.*

fume (fyüm), **1** vapor, gas, or smoke, especially if harmful, strong, or giving out odor: *The fumes from the car's exhaust nearly choked me. n.*

glad i a tor (glad′ē ā′tər), slave, captive, or paid fighter who fought at the public shows in the arenas in the ancient Roman Empire. *n.*

gran deur (gran′jər), greatness; majesty; nobility; dignity; splendor. *n.*

joust (joust *or* just), **1** combat between two knights on horseback, armed with lances. **2** fight with lances on horseback. Knights used to joust with each other for sport. 1 *n.,* 2 *v.*

lance (lans), a long, wooden spear with a sharp iron or steel head: *The knights carried lances into battle. n.*

lout (lout), an awkward, stupid person; boor. *n.*

me di e val (mē′dē ē′vəl *or* med′ē ē′vəl), of or belonging to the Middle Ages (the years from about A.D. 500 to about 1450). *adj.* Also, **mediaeval.**

me ni al (mē′nē əl), of or suited to a servant; low; mean: *Cinderella had to do menial tasks. adj.*

a	hat	**oi**	oil
ā	age	**ou**	out
ä	far	**u**	cup
e	let	**ů**	put
ē	equal	**ü**	rule
ėr	term		
i	it	**ch**	child
ī	ice	**ng**	long
o	hot	**sh**	she
ō	open	**th**	thin
ô	order	**ŧʜ**	then
		zh	measure

ə = a in about, e in taken, i in pencil, o in lemon, u in circus

medieval —a medieval nobleman, about A.D. 1250

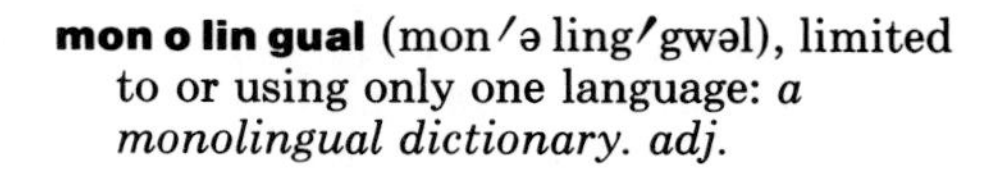

mon o lin gual (mon′ə ling′gwəl), limited to or using only one language: *a monolingual dictionary. adj.*

non com pli ance, *See* **compliance.**

o blige (ə blīj′), **1** bind by a promise, contract, duty, etc.; compel; force: *The law obliges parents to send their children to school.* **2** do a favor for: *Kindly oblige me by closing the door. v.,* **o bliged, o blig ing.**

ob nox ious (əb nok′shəs), very disagreeable; offensive; hateful: *Their rudeness and bad manners made them obnoxious to me. adj.*

rit u al (rich′ü əl), **1** a form or system of ceremonies. Baptism, marriage, and burial are parts of the ritual of most churches. Secret societies have a ritual for initiating new members. **2** of ceremonies; done as a ceremony: *a ritual dance, ritual laws. 1 n., 2 adj.*

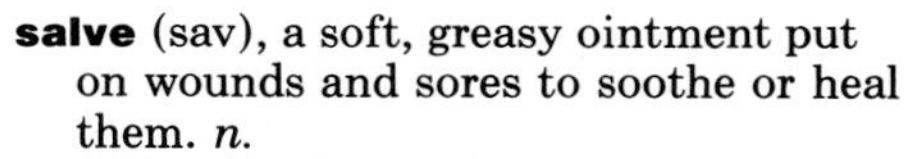

salve (sav), a soft, greasy ointment put on wounds and sores to soothe or heal them. *n.*

scab bard (skab′ərd), a sheath or case for the blade of a sword, dagger, etc. *n.*

squire (skwīr), a young man of noble family who attended a knight till he himself was made a knight. *n.*

standard (stan′dərd), of the accepted or normal size, amount, power, quality, etc.: *the standard rate of pay, a standard gauge. adj.*

sulfur

sul fur (sul′fər), a light-yellow nonmetallic element that burns easily, producing a stifling odor. Sulfur is common in volcanic regions, occurring in nature in both free and combined forms, and is also in proteins. It is used in making matches, gunpowder, paper pulp, fertilizers, insecticides, etc., and in medicine. *n.* Also, **sulphur.**

surge (sėrj), rise and fall; move like waves: *A great wave surged over us. The crowd surged through the streets. v.,* **surged, surg ing.**

tech noc ra cy (tek nok′rə sē), government by technical experts. *n.*

tech no crat (tek′nə krat), person in favor of technocracy. *n.*

tour na ment (tėr′nə mənt *or* tůr′nə mənt), **1** series of contests testing the skill of many persons in some sport: *a golf tournament.* **2** a medieval contest between two groups of knights on horseback who fought for a prize. *n.*

trem or (trem′ər), **1** an involuntary shaking or trembling: *a nervous tremor in the voice.* **2** a shaking or vibrating movement. An earthquake is sometimes called an earth tremor. *n.*

tur moil (tėr′moil), a commotion; disturbance; disorder: *Unexpected guests put us in a turmoil. n.*

va por ize (vā′pə rīz′), change into a gas called vapor: *Heat vaporizes water. v.,* **va por ized, va por iz ing.**

ver sion (vėr′zhən), one particular statement, account, or description: *Each of the three boys gave his own version of the quarrel. n.*

voy age (voi′ij), **1** a journey by water; cruise: *We had a pleasant voyage to England.* **2** a journey through the air or through space: *the earth's voyage around the sun. n.*

voy ag er (voi′i jər), person who makes a voyage; traveler. *n.*

vul ner a ble (vul′nər ə bəl), capable of being wounded or injured; open to attack: *The army's retreat left the city vulnerable. adj.*

yoke (yōk), **1** a wooden frame which fits around the necks of two work animals to fasten them together for pulling a plow or vehicle. **2** any frame connecting two other parts: *I tried to carry two buckets on a yoke, one at each end. n.*

zom bie (zom′bē), corpse supposedly brought to a trancelike condition resembling life by a supernatural power. *n., pl.* **zom bies.**

a	hat	**oi**	oil
ā	age	**ou**	out
ä	far	**u**	cup
e	let	**ů**	put
ē	equal	**ü**	rule
ėr	term		
i	it	**ch**	child
ī	ice	**ng**	long
o	hot	**sh**	she
ō	open	**th**	thin
ô	order	**ᴛʜ**	then
		zh	measure

ə = a in about, e in taken, i in pencil, o in lemon, u in circus

yoke (def.1)

ACKNOWLEDGMENTS

Text

Page 8: Chapters 1–4 from *Max and Me and the Time Machine*, copyright © 1983 by Gery Greer and Bob Ruddick, reprinted by permission of Harcourt Brace & Company.

Page 40: *Journey to Technos* by Claire Boiko from *Plays*, 1986. Copyright © 1986 by Plays, Inc. Reprinted by permission.

Page 64: "The Day the Mountain Blew Apart" by Chris Copeland from *Challenge Plus*, May 1990. Reprinted by permission of the author.

Page 75: From the book, *Pompeii: Nightmare at Midday* by Kathryn Long Humphrey, pages 11–33. Copyright © 1990 by Kathryn Long Humphrey. Reprinted by permission of the publisher, Franklin Watts, Inc.

Page 91: From *Tails of the Bronx: A Tale of the Bronx* by Jill Pinkwater, pages 9–19. Copyright ©1991 by Jill Pinkwater. Reprinted with the permission of Simon & Schuster Books for Young Readers.

Page 107: "Pioneer Children in the West" from *Children of the Wild West* by Russell Freedman. Copyright © 1983 by Russell Freedman. Reprinted by permission of Clarion Books, a Houghton Mifflin Company imprint. All rights reserved.

Page 117: "The Modern Olympics" from *Great Summer Olympic Moments* by Nate Aaseng. Copyright © 1990 by Lerner Publications Company, 241 First Avenue North, Minneapolis, MN 55401. Used by permission of the publisher.

Page 127: "Maya Ballplayers" by Peter Kvietok from *FACES* Magazine November, 1985, issue: "The Maya Civilization." © 1985, Cobblestone Publishing, Inc., 7 School Street, Peterborough, NH 03458. Reprinted by permission of the publisher.

Artists

Illustrations owned and copyrighted by the illustrator.

Cover: Wayne McLoughlin

Pages 6–7, 62–63, 88–89, 114–115: Lance Jackson

Pages 9–40: Tom Gieseke

Pages 42–62: John Hersey

Pages 90–105: Gil Ashby

Photographs

Pages 6–7: Syntax International. Page 23: Pierpont Morgan Library. Page 25: The Robert L. Metzenberg Collection/Cooper-Hewitt Museum/Gift of Eleanor L. Metzenberg, Photo courtesy Art Resource, New York. Page 49: Milt and Joan Mann/Cameramann International, Ltd. Page 56: Cameramann International, Ltd. Pages 62 bottom right–63 bottom left: David Mlotok. Pages 62 left column, 63 bottom right: U.S. Geological Survey. Page 63 top: Giraudon/Art Resource, NY. Pages 64–65: U.S.G.S. Page 66 top: U.S.D.A., photo by Jerry Franklin. Page 66 bottom: John Barr/Gamma-Liaison. Page 69 top: Official U.S. Navy Photograph. Page 69 bottom: AP/Wide World Photos Page 70: U.S.D.A., Photo Jerry Franklin. Page 72: Roger Werth, *Longview Daily News*, Woodfin Camp, Inc. Pages 80–81: Giraudon/Art Resource, NY. Page 81 top: Art Resource, NY. Page 83: top, The Bettman Archive; inset, Matthew Borkoski/West Stock. Page 85: Pompeii map by Joe LeMonnier, Viking-Penguin. Pages 86, 88: Matthew Borkoski/West Stop. Page 89: top, David Mlotok; bottom, Leonard Von Matt/Photo Researchers. Page 91: Matthew Borkoski/West Stock. Page 88: top, Beryl Goldberg; center and bottom, Syntax International. Page 89: top, Nebraska State Historical Society; bottom, The National Archives. Page 106: Courtesy of the Roy Andrews Collection, University of Oregon Library. Page 108: Idaho State Historical Society. Page 109 bottom: The National Archives. Page 109 top: Minnesota Historical Society. Page 110: Courtesy of the National Archives. Page 114: Syntax International. Page 115: left, Charles Gallenkamp, Courtesy National Museum of Anthropology, Mexico; right, American Museum of Natural History. Page 116: Bob Daemmrich. Page 117: P. Rivera/SUPERSTOCK. Page 119: The Bettman Archive. Page 123 bottom left: Dave Black. Pages 126–127: Walter Iooss, Jr., Fuji Photo Film USA. Page 128: Charles Gallenkamp, Courtesy National Museum of Anthropology, Mexico. Pages 130, 133: American Museum of Natural History. Page 134: Museum of New Mexico. Page 135: U.S. Geological Survey. Pages 126–138: Syntax International. Page 140: NASA. Page 143: Library of Congress.

Unless otherwise acknowledged, all photographs are the property of ScottForesman.

Glossary

The contents of the Glossary entries in this book have been adapted from *Scott, Foresman Intermediate Dictionary*, Copyright © 1988 by Scott, Foresman and Company, and *Scott, Foresman Advanced Dictionary*, Copyright © 1988 by Scott, Foresman and Company.